Confessions of a Cruise Ship Comedian

Written by

Dave Goodman

Edited by

Bob Kubota

Confessions of a Cruise Ship Comedian

Laughter is the greatest music!

An audience laughing is a symphony of happiness!

The laughter of children is magical!

Be careful out there! You never know who you will meet on the Lido Deck!

What to Expect

It can take a comedian 10 years to develop a GREAT 30-45 minute set. Cruise lines will ask that we do two different 45 minute shows while aboard so that they feel they have gotten the most for their money. I know of comedians who were so stressed about the obligation that it brought on visits to Emergency Room with fears of a heart attack. I handled it by talking very slowly.

In the 1980's and early 1990's comedians looked down on the ships and comedians who worked on ships. I was performing in Las Vegas from 1992 until late 1995 and was just starting to book dates on ships. At 30 I was considered pretty young for working ships.

I was about to go on stage in Las Vegas. I was hanging out behind the stage with the other comedians. We were talking about business and what we were doing the next week. I told the two comedians I was off to do another cruise in the Caribbean.

These two guys start ripping me apart verbally. "What? Now you're a boat act? Nice!", one guy said. The other asked, "Do you like babysitting old people?" For the next 5 minutes all I heard were boat jokes. These two guys roasted me for working ships. Today both of these guys are working on ships for Carnival Cruise Lines. Oh how time can change your perception!

5

If a singer falls ill or if the juggler's props did not show up you run the risk of being asked to fill in for that act. Yet a third show! Each show brings a diminishing response from the audience. As a comedian you resort to telling clean street jokes and you even go to the old standard "Hi. How ya' doin'? Where are you from?" At this point the passengers have seen the proverbial wizard behind the curtain and it now takes more to elicit the same amount of laughter as your first show.

All the while the Cruise Director is making notes on the material and using it on the next cruise that you are not performing on. Every once in a while the Cruise Director will forget whose material he stole and will perform that evening's comedian's material as he is opening the show for that very comedian!

If this happens you have to dance around the material and omit it from the show or you are the one who looks like a moron. On one occasion I actually took a breath when I was about to come to one of the jokes already performed moments earlier by the Cruise Director. I thought about what move to make so that the segue would be seamless and the passengers would not know. I took a chance and decided to say, "How about a hand for the Cruise Director. She is a very funny lady. I actually wrote all of the material she performed tonight. Sorry to say that she forgot to pay me for the material. I actually have every reason to believe it is just an oversight. She is so forgetful. So I am going to ask a favor. Can you please write a little note to the Cruise Director reminding her to pay me for the jokes? No need to worry about doing it now. Just jot it down on your comment cards when you turn them in."

The Cruise Director blew a gasket backstage. The passengers could hear her cursing at me. Nervous laughter rang out from the orchestra who were hanging out behind the curtains waiting to play me off.

I never said anything to the Cruise Director. Actually, we never spoke to each other again.

I was told by the cruise staff that over 300 comment cards mentioned the money the Cruise Director should pay the comedian. One comment card said, "The Cruise Director should get her money back!"

Confessions of a Cruise Ship Comedian

Rough Seas

Today's high tech world allows ships to outrun bad weather. A ship can avoid the 12-15 foot seas they once had to deal with.

It is no fun to be on a 900 foot ship banging in rough waters for hours on end. Imagine how that would affect the psyche of the crew and passengers.

If passengers encounter bad weather early on in a cruise they can easily forgive it by the end of a week if they end the cruise with good weather. If on the last day or two of a cruise the ship is being tossed around the passengers end their voyage on a low.

On a ship in rough waters passengers find it hard to walk a straight line, they fear that the ship will sink and of course sea sickness prevails. A ship can still be tossed around in seas as small as 3 feet when wind is factored in. The final result can be overwhelming.

I have witnessed decks full of passengers with sea sick bags, buckets, and waste baskets all suffering from sea sickness. The ship may be in constant motion for as many 5 days at a time before reaching port. Cabin stewards still have to change sheets and clean cabins, bartenders still pour cocktails and the wait staff still has to deliver food and drinks 24 hours a day. Engineers are greasing gears and keeping the ship afloat, unless you are on a Carnival Cruise Lines ship, the Cruise Director still calls bingo and at 8:00 it's show time!

I have never suffered from sea sickness so I cannot relate to how hard it must be to combat the constant nausea. Even though everyone is sick they still make it out to the show! The stage is flanked by ten waiters and waitresses on each side. They are not busy serving cocktails on nights like this.

The Cruise Director warns you to not call attention to the rough seas and ignore the fact that every other person is throwing up. The orchestra starts to play "Hot! Hot! Hot!" and the Cruise Director takes the stage where he announces, "Isn't the Captain doing a great job! He is making sure we make it back to port on time!" Then he introduces the comedian and runs back to his cabin.

There are 1,400 passengers all suffering from sea sickness and I get to share the next 50 minutes with them trying to make them laugh. The best comment I ever got from a passenger when the seas were rough: "We really liked your lecture!"

Confessions of a Cruise Ship Comedian

Making an Impression

I was working with a new agent and wanted to make a great impression. She asked that I take a gig on Dolphin Cruise Lines for two weeks. If the shows went well they would use me on the larger ships in other fleets for more money. It was going to be my foot in the door.

Dolphin Cruise Lines is no longer in business. They were a one ship operation out of Cape Canaveral, Florida. They ran ships between Cape Canaveral and The Bahamas. Not the good Bahamas you are thinking of like Nassau. Nassau offers brightly painted cafes with tropical drinks and girls in bikinis. It is the postcard photo you have seen in ads. But unfortunately Dolphin's run was to the lesser traveled Freeport. In the early nineties the action was all in Nassau.

Dolphin ran the cruise for two nights for $99 and would sell out every cruise. The ship was a poorly refurbished 1954 Greek cruise ship that no one else wanted. It was riddled with troubles and breakdowns.

The day I was leaving for Cape Canaveral I got a call from the agent. She said the ship was in dry dock. The ship had some issues with putting out too much pollution and they were going to repair the problems and put the ship back in the water in a few days. The agent told me that there was a hotel room in Cape Canaveral at the Hilton in my name and that Dolphin would pick up all the expenses including food.

The next day I woke up at the Hilton and got a call from the agent. She said they needed a few more days on the repairs and the ship will be back in the water Friday. On Thursday I got a call saying that the ship would sail on Tuesday and on Monday I got a call saying the ship would sail on Friday. I flew back to LA on Saturday having never stepped on board the Dolphin ship. I still got paid for the two weeks I spent in Cape Canaveral.

On Monday morning I called the agent in Miami and said, "I got paid in Cape Canaveral in cash by someone from the office. I am sending you your commission and wanted to talk about working the bigger ships."

Two weeks go by and I hear nothing from the agent. I called again and again and again. I finally got her on the phone and she told me, "I am afraid I cannot use you on my other ships." My heart sank. She continued, "Dolphin said that your shows were not very good. I don't think I'll be able to book you on other ships, but Dolphin wants to know if you are available next month."

It's Good to Be the Comedian

Some ships provide passenger cabins and passenger privileges. This allows a comedian to dine in all the restaurants and bars with no restrictions. Some lines will only house you in crew quarters and allow you dine during certain hours in passenger areas or restrict you to staff dining rooms below deck.

Renaissance Cruise Line Cruise Lines defined my job on the ship as 'supernumerary' which provided me with unrestricted access and privileges. Renaissance Cruise Line Cruise Lines booked me in a mini suite for each of my extended contracts. I had a queen size bed, built in cabinets, large screen TV, a huge bathroom by ship standards, desk and easy chair. I was even lucky enough to have a cabin with an unrestricted view and huge porthole.

On Carnival Cruise Lines Cruise lines you are considered a crew member and you get a crew cabin. The crew accommodations are tiny cabins measuring about 12 feet deep and 7 feet wide. This space is generally shared by two crew members. There is rarely any porthole and no natural light. This small space allows for a small bathroom with a mini sink, small toilet and a shower squeezed into a corner. There is a shower curtain but it is useless. If you are a guy my size and you try to utilize the curtain you will only wind up with that curtain sticking to your ass. This will also guarantee a small flood in your cabin.

Since this is a crew cabin there is no carpet. The floor is linoleum. The combination of linoleum and water is very much like walking on ice! Add in the fact that the ship is rocking and there were many times I wound up slipping, falling and tearing the shower curtain right off the ceiling attempting to break my fall.

On Carnival Cruise Lines you would not necessarily know where you were being accommodated. Every ship seemed to have a different policy. Some ships that did the Alaska run would give you a suite. It was always a treat on Carnival Cruise Lines where you would normally be in a crew cabin.

Sometimes you strike out completely and have to overcome what seem to be impossible obstacles. Carnival Cruise Lines's original fleet included the Tropicale. It was an old tug that was strictly used for booze cruises. A booze cruise is a three or four day cruise stopping in not too distant ports and providing extended hours at sea for drinking.

I signed on in Tampa and was told there was no key for my cabin. I asked, "How do I get in?" I was told, "The door is just unlocked. No need for a key." I asked, "What do I do about my personal property when I leave the cabin?" The young cruise staff assistant helping me said, "All of the other comedians are OK with it. Why are you being so difficult? Should I call the Cruise Director?" Before I could answer the question she picked up the phone and dialed the Cruise Director. I was still shaking my head in disbelief when I heard her say, "The comedian is being really difficult about his cabin." I walked away and headed to the purser's desk. I mentioned my dilemma to the purser and she apologized and told me the ship was sold out and there were no empty cabins. I had no choice. I had to stay in the cabin with no lock. I was so obsessed about having my luggage stolen that I barely left the cabin all week.

When you work on one particular ship over any length of time you get to know the crew and learn the shortcuts and way of life on board that ship. You learn to hook up with the Chinese guys in the laundry. For a $10 tip they will do all your laundry and dry cleaning. They earn a measly $600-$900 a month working 12-16 hour days, 7 days a week with an occasional day off for contracts lasting as long as 10 months. That $10 tip may be equal to a half a day's wages.

Some entrepreneurial crew members actually established businesses right out of their cabins. Before cell phones crew members, Filipino crew members in particular, would sell phone cards. When Carnival Cruise Lines installed new televisions with built in VCRs to help improve crew morale there were crew members who started up a movie rental business. Their cabins were literally filled from the floor to the ceiling with VCR tapes. Most were pirated copies of movies dubbed into various foreign languages and they even rented XXX titles! When their contracts ended and they were heading home the business would be sold to another crew member who would keep the doors open.

Every cruise line has a crew bar. This is a bar in a restricted area solely for the use of the crew. When I started working ships a beer in the crew bar was 75 cents. A mixed drink was $1.00. Alcoholism is rampant on every cruise ship! At these prices it is almost encouraged! They sell bottled water, cigarettes at incredibly low prices (no taxes on tobacco at sea), and snacks. The bar usually opens at 1:00 PM and stays open until 2:00 or 3:00 AM.

The crew bar is Groundhog Day every night! Get drunk, try to get laid and try to pretend what the Polish crew member was trying to say to you in her broken English. There are clicks of all types usually based on their countries of origin. Groups of Croatians all smoking and chatting a million miles a minute. The dining room waiters, who were usually Dominican, are playing Dominoes and drinking Red Stripes. At the bar would be the Italian officers dressed in their white uniforms stalking the newly signed on crew members of the opposite sex. In the back would be the entertainers, the dancers, magicians, musicians and the like.

I loved the crew bar! It was like watching a tiny version of the UN at work on the high seas. You see people of different nationalities, religions and color all coming together. I have never known there to be an incident on a ship where groups of people from one country were fighting with a group from another country. Like children on a playground (except in this case the children are holding cocktails) there are a lot of smiling faces. Oh yeah, it's the alcohol at work!

Train Wreck at Sea

My favorite cruise acts are Hypnotists! Hands down! Why you ask? Well I love to see a train wreck! I have never seen a successful hypnotist on a ship. I know a lot of successful hypnotists who work on dry land. I am not certain if the motion of the ship has an affect but I have witnessed four hypnotists working on ships over the years and never saw a show.

A hypnotist will come out on stage and start their show by speaking about hypnosis and the process you are about to witness. The hypnotist is getting the audience comfortable hearing his voice. At the same time the hypnotist is looking for good subjects that he believes he can put under.

The hypnotist is trying to engage some audience members to participate in the show by volunteering to be placed under hypnosis. Some of the volunteers are more reluctant and only participate because the hypnotist will insist they participate.

An effective hypnotist will have subjects under in a fairly short period of time. A cruise ship hypnotist will try for up to 30 minutes before conceding that not everyone who volunteers will go under. At that point the show is over and the passengers leave thinking, "What the hell did I just see?"

I worked with a balancing act one summer in Alaska. He was out of the Northwest, possibly Vancouver, Canada and was really abrasive. I avoided him 99% of the time I was working with him on a repositioning cruise. This is where the ship leaves one seasonal location and heads back to another port for the upcoming fall or spring sailing season. In this case the ship was leaving Hawaii for Alaska. The seas were 5 and 6 feet. How does a guy who balances on round objects work in high seas with a ship rocking back and forth? An even better question to me was, "How does a balancing act keep the audience's attention for 45 minutes?" I could not wait to see the show. Even though he was given a chance to opt out of the show in rough seas he insisted, "The show must go on!"

The showroom was packed with passengers. I stood in the balcony in back of the room. The orchestra starts to play. The lights go dim. The Cruise Director announces, "Are you ready for show time?" The crowd howls in response and the curtains open up. The spotlight hits the stage and the balancing act walks out and says, "Due to the rough seas I will not be able to perform this evening. Thank you very much. Thank you very much. Thank you very much. Good night!" And he walked off stage.

Here is the 1% where I did not avoid him. In the officer's mess the next morning I asked him, "Why did you not bow out of the show earlier in the day?" He said, "I wanted to make sure I would get paid."

On ships there are several singers. These singers are usually female and traditionally very attractive. Some sing in the lounge, others in the disco and some only perform in the main show room as headliners in various production shows.

When I was working at Princess Cruise Line I became friends with one of the singers, Nikki, who was from England. She was finishing her contract and heading to Utah to marry her American boyfriend. We were on the same flight to Miami so we shared a cab to the airport. Nikki was overloaded with luggage and spent the majority of her time that morning whisking items out of one bag and into another.

We get checked in and head to security. We placed our bags on the X-ray belt and headed through the scanner. I was ahead of Nikki and was just collecting my stuff when she got pulled aside with her bag. A group of security officers are now surrounding the X-ray image of Nikki's bag. From where I am standing there is a clear shot of the screen. Right there on the screen, there in big bold black and white image is a huge dildo! One officer pulled the bag off the belt and opened the bag. He reached inside and pulled out the dildo waiving it over his head as if in victory.

Even though it was early in the morning the airport was packed and everyone was laughing.

I was a little embarrassed that people would think we were a couple. So I scurried away as quickly as possible while Nikki was yelling at me, "Don't worry, Honey! They don't think you can't satisfy me." It sounded so eloquent in an English accent.

Just My Preference

Stay away from the mega ships. Sail on the smaller and more intimate ships in the 700 – 1200 passengers range. You will spend less time in line and more time enjoying your cruise.

By traveling on a smaller ship you considerably reduce your exposure to all kinds of craziness including ship borne diseases that may keep you in the bathroom for hours if not days. In the last 10 years there have been numerous outbreaks even on the best of cruise lines. It is unavoidable. Sometimes the crew is ground zero for these outbreaks and sometimes it's the passengers who are responsible. No matter what the origin is I have never been exposed to this and I am very thankful.

The major difference in ship size from large to small is revenue. The larger the ship is the more revenue they need to generate. If a ship has 3,500 passengers you will have more sea days just so that the company can generate sales in the gift shops, revenue in the casino and of course the millions of dollars that the bars bring in daily!

Here is the best scenario for why you should sail on a small ship. If you would stand in line at a purser's desk for help with your cabin or at the shore excursion counter to book a trip you might wait 15 minutes in line on a ship with 1,200 passengers. If you are on a ship with 3,500 passengers that same wait would be close to 45 minutes.

Now think about how many lines you are going to stand in over the course of the cruise. You stand in line to get on the ship and to get off the ship. You stand in line to be seated in the dining room and you stand in line at the buffet. You have to stand in line to get your passport checked and you have to wait in line to clear customs. You have to dance in the Conga line that wraps around the dining room which is a whole new line and instead of standing you dance but it is still a line! You have to stand in line at the bar and you have to stand in line to get into the showroom. When you sign up for a tour you have stand in line with your group. This is why they call it a CRUISE LINE!

Going Commando

When performing on cruise ships you become very acquainted with what I call Travel Survival Skills. Cruise Lines fly you into airports around the world and it is up to you to get on the right flights, clear customs and get yourself to the ship before it sails. There are occasions where a ship's agent will meet you at the airport and transport you to the ship or to the hotel you may be spending the night at. There are times when you are left to your own Travel Survival Skills.

I flew into Panama to get on a ship repositioning to Hawaii for the spring. First the ship had to pass through the Panama Canal. These trips through the Panama Canal were notorious for having the oldest passengers at sea. The reason for that reputation was that the ship had extended sea days. The itinerary would only allow for a handful of ports on a two week cruise. Most seniors do not care for the daily on and off that younger passengers love about sailing in Europe.

According to my travel documents and my airline tickets I could not figure out how I was getting on or off the ship. It would not be the first time the office made an error in my travel arrangements to meet a ship. I went over the information again and again and could not make any sense of the situation. I woke up in the hotel to find other acts needing to get to the ship including a musician I knew named Billy.

I was informed that the four of us would take a jeep ride through the jungle to Cologne, Panama and jump on a pilot boat. A pilot boat is used to ferry customs officials on ships and to help guide ships into port and to the proper berth.

We get to Cologne and hand our bags over to a guy on a horrible little wooden boat with chipped paint and rubbish everywhere. Not the pilot boat I envisioned when we were told pilot boat! Billy, one of the guys traveling with us, was a well seasoned veteran of the trip we were taking. Billy looked over at me while we were tooling along in the rain in an open boat and said, "You are going to love climbing the cargo net into the ship!" I thought he was kidding but the closer we got to the ship the more information was revealed and the more I realized Billy was telling the truth.

I was told that the ship is moving and we pull alongside the ship and they throw a cargo net out the cargo door and we climb up into the ship. The pilot boat we were on was maybe 25 feet long and 8 feet wide. The cruise ship we were expected to pull up alongside of without being crushed was 895 feet long and 12 stories tall. The math equation going on in my head was X + Y = Dave's a dead man!

What in the world were they thinking when they made these plans for me? I have a fear of heights! I have vertigo! I can't do this!

Do you look at me and see a Navy Seal? Do you see an Army Commando? I see a great big pussy!

I was going to quit right there on the pilot boat but the ride back to Cologne on the pilot boat was just as iffy as me climbing the cargo net. Two guys, much more adept and physically fit than me, hurried up the net without issue. They made it look easy. The next to go up was Billy who was 75. Billy was making fun of me as he went up the cargo net said, "I gotta see you climb that cargo net from this perspective!"

The pilot boat is now smacking against the side of the ship and the crew members who are assisting us are now yelling for us to hurry up. Apparently the ship needed to speed up to avoid the traffic in the mouth of the Panama Canal. To say I was nervous, freaking out, panic stricken or even overcome with fear would be nowhere near what I was really experiencing.

I grabbed the cargo net and climbed for the outstretched hand of one of the Boson's who did not fear me dragging him over board! Once on the ship I was literally shaking and needed a moment to get myself together.

The Crew Purser met us at the cargo door as we were collecting our luggage. She welcomed us aboard and gave us the news that we would be leaving the ship in two days the same way we got on!

For forty-eight hours I did not sleep. I was consumed with fear about having to climb that cargo net again. I begged the Crew Purser to call the office in Miami to change my travel plans and send me home from Costa Rica. All of my requests were denied.

I got dressed for my show headed to the backstage area. The Cruise Director showed up to introduce the show. He said that every passenger was lined up at the rails to watch us climb aboard. I guess that was the highlight of the day.

I opened my show that night by asking, "How many people watched me climb the cargo net to get here?" Just about everyone in the showroom applauded. I said, "I never risked my life to tell jokes to an audience before so you better really appreciate this show!"

Forty-eight hours later I am standing at the door with the same four guys who climbed aboard with me. They all had a good laugh at my expense knowing how frightened I was. The four guys agreed to let me go down first. As I was throwing my leg over the side of the cargo door I hear the Billy, the 75 year old musician say, "Let him go first. This way we won't have to break his fall."

Sure enough I got disoriented and missed the last four rungs of the cargo net and landed flat on my back on deck of the pilot boat looking up at the crew in the open cargo door laughing at me. I stood up and did a quick inventory of my important parts and realized I was just shook up from the fall. I looked up at the ship and saw passengers lined up at the rails applauding the fact I was OK.

Role Reversal

I got a call from a friend who had just started working for Renaissance Cruise Line Cruise Lines in Europe. At this point, the only line I was working for was Carnival Cruise Lines. My land gigs were keeping me busy but I would love the chance to work in Europe. I got a number to an agent in New York who was booking comedians for Renaissance Cruise Line. I sent over my promo stuff and got a call to fly to Barcelona for a month on the R2.

The agent for Renaissance Cruise Line was a nut job! She sent me all the travel documents and spent excessive amounts of time explaining how I should behave and what I should do. I am an adult and have experience working on ships and I did not need to be coached. Each time we spoke she handled the call as if she believed I was not really committed to getting on the plane. I had to calm her down by confirming I was committed. There were several conversations over the course of a week where she expressed the same anxiety ridden thoughts again and again.

The day before I left for the airport I got one more call from the agent. She was busy repeating herself on all the previous points we had discussed. There was one new wrinkle. She made it very clear that she did not want me on that ship discussing my salary with anyone. Her warning was a huge red flag. Why is it that she would bring this up? I have never had a discussion with an agent who would dictate such things. Something was not right.

The first show on this five-day cruise was a magician, Rory, who worked with his wife, Kat. The act was good. The crowd loved them. Kat would dress up as an English Sheep Dog and assist Rory doing card tricks. After their first show we met in the crew bar. I found them to be a great couple and fun to talk show biz with. We knew a lot of the same people from Las Vegas where we had all once lived. It was a nice friendship.

On the second night I performed, after the show, there was a noticeable difference in the way I was being treated by the crew and staff. Suddenly I was very popular in the crew bar. It was as if the entire crew had been watching the show to determine if they were going to be friendly with me only if I was funny. Crew and staff would compliment me and shake my hand to welcome me to the ship. It was fun and something I never experienced before.

That night in the crew bar Rory told me that each of the headline acts on the ships were making the same money. Rory warned me that he knew who my agent was and warned me to be very careful. Rory swore up and down that the money was about $600.00 more a week than I was getting paid. Not only was I being shorted $600.00 a week,

I was also paying a 15% commission! Now I know why she did not want me to talk to anyone about my contract!

The next day the ship stopped in Malaga, Spain. I got off the ship and found a payphone. I used my Sprint calling card and got my agent on the phone. I told her that the shows went great and I was really happy about the cabin and access that Renaissance Cruise Line allowed me. I then told her that I had to fill out some paperwork on the ship and found out that I got a raise! She asked me how that came to be. I said that the accounting department from Paramount Productions sent a 1099 Tax form to the ship for me fill out and attached were the details of the contract for my month on the ship.

I could hear my agent breathing heavy and not knowing what to say. I continued to tell her that the numbers were $600.00 more a week than we discussed so that meant she was going to get a bigger commission check! She balked, stuttered and caved in that she must have made a mistake! I congratulated her on her $90.00 pay increase and hung up the phone.

I continued to work with the same agent keeping both of my eyes on the money. Later in the year I found out that she had booked my roommate, who was also a comedian, for 50% of what the budget allowed for. Even though he knew better he also needed the work. She also booked another comedian I knew for about $1,000.00 a week less than the budget. She developed a plan which enabled her to rob comedians.

The agent would have the production company (in this case the production company was Paramount Productions which was a subsidiary of the studio) directly send her your check and she in turn determined what portion of that check she wanted you to have. It was easy for her to get away with this as she asked comedians to sign power of attorney contracts in order to deposit the checks. She in turn would wire an amount to the comedian's bank account. If you refused to sign she simply would not do business with you. She got away with this for years. Last I heard she is still in the business of booking comedians.

Moon River

My regular routine for a few months was meeting up with my friend Denny at LAX on Thursdays. Denny was also working at Carnival Cruise Lines as a singer and musician and was the opening act on show nights. We were always booked on the same flights to Mazatlan, Mexico. Denny had been doing this route for Carnival Cruise Lines for years and when the ships repositioned to Alaska for the summer, Denny would fly between Alaska and Mexico every week for the entire summer season. It was exhausting but financially rewarding. As an added bonus Denny collected millions of miles on his frequent flyer account with Alaska and earned a coveted elite status with the airline that allowed for unlimited first class upgrades almost other perks.

As soon as I would arrive at the gate Denny would grab my ticket and run to the counter to get me upgraded too. We would sit in first class drinking for 3 hours all the way to Mazatlan. We developed a standard plan on every trip. We would meet up at LAX. I would get upgraded by Denny. We would devour all the Corona and Cuervo they served in first class. Denny would tell me jokes all flight long and his favorite was,

"Two guys on a deserted island. They are never going to be rescued. One guy turns to the other and says, 'We are never

35

getting off this island and I am horny. How about we have sex?'

His buddy freaks out and says, 'No way!'

But the first guy keeps begging him. He sweetens the deal by offering this, 'If you don't like it make animal noises and if you do like it sing a song!'

His buddy gives in and they begin and his buddy starts to scream, 'Moo! Moo! Moo! Moooon river!'

When we land in Mazatlan we had a driver who would meet us the airport he would take us to the ship. We would get our cabin assignments and drop off our luggage. We would then turn around and leave the ship to head to the Shrimp Bucket and have lunch for two hours. When we ordered a Corona the waiter would bring a metal bucket loaded with beers! Best happy hour in Mazatlan! By 6:00 we would head back to the ship with plans of meeting at the casino bar at 10:00.

There were a few summers when Denny and I shared the burden of flying between Mexico and Alaska. We made the most of it. While we were in Alaska there were no drunken exploits. The passengers on ships in Alaska tend be in bed by ten so the night life just isn't there. Denny also had an extra set of shows on the ship where he sang 50's tunes in the showroom with back up dancers.

In all the years I worked with Denny I never went out to see that show until my last trip to Alaska. I did not know this would be my last Alaska trip but it turned to be a disastrous one.

I got to the showroom and stood in the very back of the balcony as I always did. The dancers were finishing a number and Denny was about to come to center stage and start his show. I noticed the dancers were exiting on a hydraulic stage that lowered to the deck below. At the same time Denny came out from the wings headed to center stage. The lighting crew never hit him with the spot and lights remained dark from the end of the previous dance number. Denny never knew that the hydraulic stage was not returned to the proper position and he fell right into the gaping hole in the floor.

I was frozen for a good thirty seconds thinking, "Did that just happen?" The house lights came on and they announced for the showroom to evacuate in a calm fashion. Over the public address system you could hear the code being called for an emergency in the showroom.

I ran from the upper balcony of the ship to the crew entrance behind the stage and down the three flights of stairs to the deck below the stage where Denny fell. By the time I got there dancers were limping away and crying hysterically. Denny had landed on few on them but thankfully none were hurt badly. The same could not be said for Denny. He was in serious pain lying in a contorted position on top of equipment from the band and miscellaneous props.

I was asked to leave the immediate area by the emergency team on board the ship. The emergency team is comprised of volunteers from various departments and of course the ships' doctor and nursing staff. They train for situations like this and I was praying Denny would be OK.

I decided to head to the infirmary where they would eventually bring Denny. They arrived and kept everyone from entering the clinic. Every few minutes a nurse would poke her head out the door and say that he was doing OK.

Eventually the emergency team members headed back to their jobs and the area outside the clinic was mobbed with dancers, musicians and tech crew members who all were concerned for Denny.

A nurse came out and asked, "Is Dave Goodman here?"

I answered and the nurse told me that Denny wanted to see me. I headed into the clinic to see Denny on his back with oxygen, his leg was draped and the staff was busy attending to him. Denny asked me to help out and keep an eye on his personal items as he knew they would be flying him off the ship to a hospital.

The doctor interrupted our conversation. He spoke in very broken English and turned out to be a Spanish National.

He told Denny in his spectacularly poor English, "Inin denchick anele.'

Denny said, "I don't understand."

The doctor repeated, "Inin denchick anele."

After repeating himself twice more I realized that he was telling Denny, "I need to check your anus!"

Denny let out a huge laugh which made me feel better. Now the doctor asks me to help roll Denny over so he can proceed. Denny's face is literally an inch from my face. The doctor warns Denny that he is about to begin and Denny tells the doctor to go right ahead.

As the doctor performs his exam Denny clenches and starts to say, "Moo! Moo! Mooooon River!"

I laughed so hard and uncontrollably that the nurses asked me to step outside.

Ultimately, Denny was very banged up and was never able to return to work again. Carnival Cruise Lines refused to pay for his care, hospital bills and they certainly did not compensate him financially for the work he had to miss. Eventually Denny hired a lawyer out of Long Beach, California who specialized in maritime law.

It is very difficult to sue a cruise line in the United States. Most ships are registered in Panama and other countries where they feast on the tax money they avoid paying to the United States and remain protected under international law.

Denny's lawyer contacted me to be a witness at a deposition prior to trial. One week later I received a call from the lawyers for Carnival Cruise Lines who had offices in San Diego, California. I was asked by a female lawyer if I was aware of the deposition and if I was willing to give testimony.

The lawyer said to me, "We need to make sure that we get our story out there so that we do not pay this Denny guy a penny! We are on team Carnival Cruise Lines and we want to make sure that you are too!"

I was blown away! I did not know how to respond and I found myself being righteous.

I said, "Look lady I intend to tell the truth! I am on team truth! I am not sure if you are aware that I was called to be a witness by Denny's lawyer. I no longer work for Carnival Cruise Lines and have not worked for them in years. I now have a moral obligation to inform Denny's lawyers as to the exact nature of this phone call. Have a good day."

I was served a summons that I was a "hostile" witness and that I needed to show up at the deposition. In a conference room there was one lawyer from Carnival Cruise Lines, a stenographer and Denny's lawyer, Tom. I was asked the same questions in various forms for three and half hours. They made accusations that Denny was a drunk and a drug addict. They tried to assassinate his character and my character and that was enough for me. I asked if I could speak freely before having to leave to go about my day.

I was granted permission from both sides and I spoke honestly and emotionally about the circus they were dragging me into. I told them that Denny was not a drunk. Not a drug addict but a loyal musician who made Carnival Cruise Lines his career for 15 years or more. He was invested in Carnival Cruise Lines in every respect. He delivered great shows and was an amazing ambassador for Carnival Cruise Lines and in turn Carnival Cruise Lines denies taking care of an error made by a crew member who worked on the tech crew in the showroom.

I made certain to address the phone call I received from Carnival Cruise Lines' lawyer and got that on record after strong protest from Carnival Cruise Lines' lawyer. I got in every sordid detail that she did not want to be responsible for. I found myself protecting my friend who can now only walk with the use of a cane.

I said, "He is in chronic pain and his insurance will not cover the cost of the surgery he needs. Carnival Cruise Lines needs to do the right thing. Denny was hurt as the result of an accident while on a ship working for Carnival Cruise Lines and now his life has changed forever."

I got really emotional. I felt like Denny was going to get screwed and the corporate world was going to win.

A few days later I got a call from Denny and his lawyer, Tom. They received a significant settlement from Carnival Cruise Lines. They could not disclose details of the settlement but several weeks later Denny got his check and took me out to lunch in his brand new $100,000.00 BMW.

Insomnia

It sounds like a dream to live on a luxury cruise ship sailing around the world and it is every bit as exciting as it sounds. Although traveling alone to romantic destinations is very depressing. You see couples kissing at the Trevi Fountain and you are alone. You see couples having their photos taken in front of the Sphinx and you are alone. You see families in trattorias dining and laughing and you are alone. The road can be very lonely and monotonous.

I was on the R5 for Renaissance Cruise Line. The ship was going to sail from Istanbul to Athens with stops in Cyprus, Israel, Egypt, Turkey, Greece and occasional trips to the Ukraine, Bulgaria and Romania via the Black Sea. I was on this run from September 2000 until January 2001. I loved the cities we stopped in. These were the cities I read about in geography class and the cities I dreamed of one day traveling to.

The first three months on that run and I spent every day in town shopping, dining and hanging out with the crew. I grew to love Pireaus, Greece and knew where to find the best feta and pita. In Rhodes, Greece I can bring you to an amazing Gyros stand that I ate at every time we stopped in Rhodes. In Istanbul there is a 125 year old restaurant off Taksim Square named Haci Abdullahs. An amazing restaurant serving old world delights like lamb in béchamel

43

sauce and pickled everything! We did 4 overnight stays in Istanbul and I would dine twice a day at Haci Abdullahs. The waiters did not speak English and I spoke no Turkish but they welcomed me each time I showed up with a smile and a handshake. To this day I find Turks to be great, fun loving people.

This was my life and as exciting as it was I was not functioning well. I was very lonely. Having my girlfriend 8,000 miles away was wearing me down. Not being in touch with my friends was tough. Not having seen my mail in months was tough. For Christ's sake I missed Diet Coke! Not being in tune with who won the World Series was tough. On this particular year the New York Yankees were playing the New York Mets. I dreamed about a subway series when I was a kid growing up in New York and it finally happened. Only I was in Europe and did not see one game!

I was only doing one show a week giving me way too much down time. I had not been sleeping. I was taking cat naps but certainly not sleeping through the night. I was wandering the ship at all hours of the day and night. The security officers would be doing their rounds and find me in the crew bar or staffs mess at four in the morning and ask if I had been to bed yet. I starting to feel run down and beat up.

On our next stop to Istanbul I went to a pharmacist and asked for Valium to help me sleep. (In Europe getting "prescription" medication over the counter is less of a hassle than the United States.) The pharmacist literally chuckled and said he could not prescribe such strong drugs without a prescription but he did suggest something that came in a little brown bottle in a little white box with Roche Labs across the top of the bottle.

It was $45.00 for fifty pills and I paid in Turkish Lira which was literally $32,000,000 Turkish Lira. At $800,000 Turkish Lira to the dollar you had to be a math whiz in order to convert the costs of anything in Turkey to dollars. I got back to the ship at 6:00 PM after my dinner at Haci Abdullah. At 8:00 I took two Lexotanils. The packaging was in German and I had no idea what the dosage was. I could have asked one of the German speaking crew members but experimenting can be more fun.

I woke up 18 hours later! I had found my cure! I did not abuse the pills and they indeed lasted for a long time! Almost two months! You do the math!

That prescription made it all the way to Tokyo. I was flying home from Tokyo with buddy and fellow comedian Bob Kubota. We had just finished three weeks of USO shows in Korea and we were exhausted. We were counting the days to get home and finally we were changing planes from Seoul to Tokyo and heading back to LAX.

Once on the plane I offered Bob one of my two remaining Lexotanils. Bob quickly accepted my offer.

I got a glass of water and downed my pill and said to Bob, "See you in Los Angeles."

I woke up and looked at my watch. Eight hours had gone by! I slept eight of nine hours all the way back to LAX!

I turned to Bob and said, "Hey, One more hour!"

Bob said, "Look out the window, Dave. We have not left Tokyo!"

A Typhoon moved into Tokyo before we could take off. They kept us on the plane on the tarmac for 8 hours! I wasted my last sleeping pill! Now I am going to be awake all the way back to LA!

When we finally lifted off from Tokyo Bob tapped me on the shoulder and said, "Thanks again for the pill!"

He swallowed it right in front of me! Bob slept all the way back to LA and I watched him sleep for nine hours!

I tried to get the same prescription again and again and always failed. I recently found out that Lexotanil is not a sleeping pill but an anxiety medication! So I was not suffering from insomnia but rather ailing from anxiety!

Mike the Trumpet Player

You have got to be careful who you talk to on ships! It is a small world and everyone knows each other.

I was working on a ship with a great group of really young musicians who played in the showroom orchestra on the Elation. They were fun loving guys who were very close off stage. They ran together as a group in port and could often be found in the crew bar together.

One night telling stories in the crew bar one of guys insisted that Mike, the trumpet player, had a great story to share. Mike had gotten into trouble with the headline act on the ship a few months earlier. The headliner was a bird trainer with trained parrots and other exotic birds. Each time one of the birds would accomplish a trick they were rewarded with a few seeds and nuts from the trainer.

The orchestra would back up the bird act and there was a rehearsal that Mike, the trumpet player, missed. The headliner was so angry that he reported Mike to the Cruise Director and Mike got written up for missing the rehearsal. If any crew member has too many written reprimands they would be fired.

Mike had a plan to retaliate against the headliner. Mike loaded his tuxedo pockets with sunflower seeds from the buffet's salad bar. Just prior to the headliner's first show in the ship's theater, with over 1,200 passengers waiting for the curtain to go up, Mike started to scatter handfuls of sunflower seeds on the stage floor.

Mike goes back to his seat and the orchestra begins to play intro music for the Cruise Director. The Cruise Director spends a few minutes telling jokes while crunching sunflower seeds under his shoes. The entire time the band is hysterical with laughter in anticipation of what is going to happen when the bird act comes out. Meanwhile the Cruise Director thinks he is doing great with the band and that his jokes are killing.

Through the curtains comes the bird trainer holding his favorite and most loyal parrot. As the bird trainer tries to pull off his first trick, the parrot is too distracted by the seeds lining the stage and is ignoring the trainer. The parrot finally flies to the stage floor for a snack. The band is laughing even harder.

Now the bird trainer grabs another bird and that bird too becomes distracted by the seeds on the stage. Finally the entire flock of trained birds and parrots fly from their perch to the goodies all over the stage. The trainer could not regain control of the birds and the show lasted 5 minutes before they closed the curtains.

Mike got written up again.

Confessions of a Cruise Ship Comedian

About a year later I was sailing on a different ship when Sloane, a horn player from the Elation, popped up out of nowhere on the Destiny. I had just boarded the Destiny and was chatting with the Cruise Director I had never met before, Corey.

Corey and Sloane were quite friendly. Sloane told me that there were a bunch of guys on the ship from the Elation that I knew. I asked if Mike the trumpet player was one of them and I got a suspicious look from Sloane but I did not pay close enough attention.

I proceed to tell Corey, the Cruise Director, about how Mike got even with the bird trainer. As I am telling the story, I get an uneasy feeling and look over Sloane who is covering his face. I then turn to Corey who is awkwardly smiling and shaking his head affirmatively.

Corey said, "Yeah. I know the story. I used to be a bird trainer performing on Carnival Cruise Lines ships before I became a Cruise Director. I even know Mike. That story might even be about me!"

I should have kept my mouth shut!

I recently heard that Corey passed away. He was a nice man and very gracious.

Confessions of a Cruise Ship Comedian

Not so Bora Bora

Renaissance Cruise Line had a deal with the French government to operate two cruise ships from Papete, Tahiti to the outer islands of Bora Bora, Huahine, Raitea and Morea. I was lucky enough to make two trips to Tahiti and I loved every second of being in the land of the $10.00 Diet Coke! Yes, a Diet Coke in the soda machine at the Sheraton was $10.00! A cheeseburger was $45.00 from room service and for breakfast bagels and lox were $69.00! The room was $899.00 a night and my room service bill alone was over $500.00. I got stuck for three extra nights! Thankfully, it was covered by Renaissance Cruise Line.

Getting in stuck in Tahiti was quite common. There was only one flight a day from Los Angeles on Air Tahiti Nui. It was the only airline I ever traded an upgrade to first class in exchange for a carton of cigarettes.

I was warned before leaving that I should pack everything I need as prices in Tahiti are some of the highest in the world due to the cost of shipping to a remote island. Most locals eat local and shop local. I did not see a McDonalds, Burger King or any other fast food restaurant. There were no franchised sit down restaurants like Outback or Dennys. No Starbucks! No Wal-Mart! No drive-thru windows!

This was truly paradise.

The ship would dock in Papete, the largest city in Tahiti. At night the local food trucks would come out by the dozens and park right outside the gangway of the ship. They offered food from all over the world. Chinese, Japanese, Italian, Indonesian, Burgers, hot dogs, and a million other choices I could not recognize. It was the hub of all the action once the sun went down. Locals would come out to dine and the more adventurous passengers would give it a go. This scene was going to be the only big city-like experience I had while in Tahiti.

This particular cruise is all about the sun and the beach and the tropical locale. There are no ruins, art museums or churches that are a must-see in Tahiti. The excitement is right outside your window. Most passengers spend the days relaxing on the beach or taking a snorkel cruise to reefs around the islands.

The one thing that hits you as soon as you get off the plane is the advertising for Tahitian Pearls. It is everywhere. On the ships they even had a local pearl vendor set up shop. Some of the strands of pearls went for as much as $60,000.00. Prices on pearls varied like the prices of diamonds. It depended on the color, the shape and a wide variety of other criteria.

The family that ran the pearl shops on the ships was very generous to the crew members at Renaissance Cruise Line.

They nurtured a fantastic relationship with the Cruise Line. The family had invited a bunch of the production show performers, tech crew and band to lunch at their home on an island only accessible by boat. I was also invited to tag along. I had never met these people before but I was encouraged to feel welcome and attend the lunch.

We were picked up by boat and taken to their little island. It almost looked like the set of Gilligan's Island. There was a little house that was completely open to the elements with three open walls. They had a huge fire pit, picnic tables and a full blown outdoor dining room table and chairs. There were about 12 of us for lunch and they served fresh tuna sashimi, coconut salad and octopus. It was fantastic!

After lunch they brought out a huge box with a lock on it. They opened the box and took out a black satin bag loaded with Tahitian Pearls. Their family had been farming pearls for decades. The family patriarch was a Frenchman who married a Tahitian girl. They remained in Tahiti and raised a family and created a pearl empire. It was surprising to see how modest a home and lifestyle they lived.

Through the trumpet player in the band, who was French Canadian and spoke French, we were told that the pearls were ours to buy at prices that amounted to pennies on the dollar when compared with prices in the shops. We spent hours picking and matching and discussing the prices via our French speaking trumpet player.

As the day was ending and we were saying goodbye I asked the trumpet player to pass on a message in French to the family patriarch. I asked for him to thank the family for their hospitality and their food and their pearls and my deepest apologies for not being able to speak French so that I may thank them myself.

As the message was being translated this wonderful, sophisticated, white haired man grabbed my face with both hands and with a smile on his face said something in French.

Our trumpet player interpreted what he said as follows, "With a smile as big as yours and with a face as big as the full moon that says it all! You need not speak French to understand that! Your soul is smiling!"

Hands down! The best part of France is Tahiti!

The Irony

Carnival Cruise Lines would fly me to Cozumel, Mexico quite often. The ships were docked until midnight and I would fly all day from LAX to Houston to Cancun and then one 9 minute flight over to Cozumel. The plane to Cozumel was dodgy. There were nine seats on this puddle jumper. Each time I did this trip I was the only passenger on the Air Caribé flight. Once you were seated, you were handed a can of fruit punch and a package of cookies by the Flight Attendant/Pilot.

The landing strip in Cozumel was an unmanned tower. The pilot had to communicate over the radio that he was landing while keeping a close eye on the airspace to make sure no other planes were in his path. It was unnerving and to boot I did this 9 minute flight without a seatbelt! Not to say that the seat belt did not fit but that it did not work! On two occasions I had the pilot signal to me if I could see anything out my side of the plane! Suddenly I was a navigator!

I landed in Cozumel at 10:00 PM and headed to the ship. I signed on and gave my passport to the Security Officers at the gangway. This was standard procedure on all Carnival Cruise Lines ships.

On Carnival Cruise Lines ships there are large numbers of security officers. Most Carnival Cruise Lines ships have dozens of security officers, usually from India. Their presence is to help maintain decorum when everyone is drunk and they certainly let their presence be known.

On Renaissance Cruise Line the ship's security team was comprised of three well-dressed officers whose uniforms made them look like ship's officers. On Renaissance Cruise Line, all security officers were retired Gurkhas from Nepal who had served in the English Army. Gurkhas are very well trained soldiers who were famous for being able to hide in the jungle well enough to reach out and touch enemy soldiers without being detected. They were highly trained killers. They were also the nicest men on earth who loved to smile, laugh and invite you to Nepal to visit them.

On certain Carnival Cruise Lines cruises, like Christmas and Spring Break, the ships would actually hire additional security officers from companies Wackenhut Security. This was always a preparation when they were expecting large numbers of college-age kids to be sailing.

I got my cabin key and went right to bed. At 3:00 in the morning I got a phone call from Raj, the head of security, who asked that I come to the security office. Once there I found out that my passport was lost between the gangway and the Crew Purser's office. This was being taken very seriously and at 3:30 in the morning they had a team of officers scouring the offices and gangway security area for my passport.

I was told to go back to bed and do not worry about it. At 8:00 in the morning the Cruise Director, Corey, called me to ask me to come to his office. He explained that the passport situation was a big problem and they were going to make announcements to the passengers offering a $500 reward for returning the passport. As we were sitting in Corey's office he found out that several other passports disappeared as well. He had to go meet with the Captain and security officers to determine what to do.

The announcements made offering a reward yielded no benefits. The next day they sweetened the offer to $1,000.00. Still no passport was returned. We had to contact the office in Miami from the ship to determine how to get me back to the United States without a passport.

The next day, the day I was signing off and returning to Los Angeles, I still had no passport. Someone from the office in Miami assured the Crew Purser that there would be a ship's representative to meet me at the airport in Miami and have me escorted through immigration. First I had to convince the Government of Grand Cayman to allow me to fly out of Georgetown, post September 11th security, without my passport.

I spent an hour in Grand Cayman explaining that my passport was stolen or lost on the Carnival Cruise Lines Destiny. They took my driver's license and social security number with them as they did a computer check.

They eventually let me get on the plane with the caveat "Do not expect getting into United States to be as easy!" They put their immigration stamp on my airline ticket!

I landed in Miami mid-afternoon. I went to passport control and explained my situation. No Carnival Cruise Lines representative and no special treatment for me. I spent 16 hours in Miami waiting to be cleared. Ultimately I was allowed entry when I explained I was leaving in four days to entertain the troops in Asia. They checked a military database where I had been listed for clearance on previous trips and they helped me get on the next flight to Los Angeles.

As soon as I got back to Los Angeles I had to head to the Federal Building on Wilshire in Santa Monica to replace my passport. The Federal building was close to my apartment and I got there early in the morning. I applied for the new passport and paid for expedited service. I had my new passport in 48 hours.

The day before I was leaving for Asia I got a call from Corey, the Cruise Director on the Destiny, who told me that they found my passport and all the missing passports. Corey told me that a security guard was caught stashing the passports in books in the ship's library. He admitted that he was selling the passports in Mexico for $500 each. Corey told me that the security guard who stole the passports was fired.

Carnival Cruise Lines refused to reimburse me for my replacement.

If you can't trust security, who can you trust?

Confessions of a Cruise Ship Comedian

62

Did That Really Just Happen?

I quit working for Carnival Cruise Lines on Christmas Eve, 2004. I walked off the ship 5 minutes prior to the ship leaving the Port of Long Beach, California, for a holiday cruise.

I had flown to Mexico to join the Paradise for Carnival Cruise Lines. I was taking the ship from Mexico back to Long Beach and then out the same day for a five-day cruise to Mexico. We referred to these trips as "front end" and "back end" trips. The "front end" was joining the ship in a US port and flying back home from a foreign city. When working the "back end" you would fly to a locale and take the ship back to a US port. The advantage to booking a trip with this type of routing meant you did not have to fly as much and you did not have to pack and unpack your bags as often.

My biggest fear going back to work for Carnival Cruise Lines at the time was that I had quit smoking and avoiding smokers and cheap cigarettes on a cruise ship are impossible. I did not want to be tempted so I was spending the majority of my time in my cabin and avoiding the crew bar.

On show night I had finished my set and headed to the crew bar for a Diet Coke. I was still in my suit with my tie dangling and my shirt soaked with perspiration when the

Cruise Director asked to speak with me. He was a Cruise Director I had never worked with before. I had never heard of his name and had no information to go on as to what kind of a guy I was dealing with. I had met him for the first time ten minutes before my show earlier in the night. To this day I do not even remember his name but I do remember he was Canadian.

I sat down at a high top table and the Cruise Director said, "I checked the computers and see that there is very little information on you in the system."

I had no idea what he was referring to. Later I learned that there was a data base of information on all of the acts Carnival Cruise Lines used on their ships.

This Cruise Director started to quiz me. "Why do you only work for Carnival Cruise Lines occasionally?"

I told him, "I was busy working gigs on dry land."

He asked, "Can you make any money doing that?"

I said, "You can make considerably more than a cruise line would pay and you get to sleep in your own bed more often."

He looked right at me and asked, "How much can you make?"

I said, "If I told you how much you would think I was lying."

He said, "I already think you are lying."

He went on to say, "What does matter is that some of your material is really inappropriate, especially sailing on Christmas. On Christmas cruises we tend to have a large Jewish crowd and they will find you very offensive. You have to stop doing any material referencing Jews."

The Cruise Director then began to list the material in my act that he did not want me to perform. Considering that I mention Judaism once in a 45 minute show I was surprised to hear his list of material I was not to perform.

Here I was with 15 years of experience performing in every imaginable venue there is for a comedian including television and some really bad movie roles. I had worked in Las Vegas and did thousands of shows. I had worked all over the US in comedy clubs. I performed on military bases around the world and did shows standing on tanks for the Marines. With all of that experience, I was never once told by anyone that my material was offensive. I was never edited by anyone at anytime and, believing in the freedom of speech, I was not going to be edited now. I was hired to entertain and not offend! I was furious and wanted to tell this guy off. I bit my lip and kept my mouth shut. I looked right into his eyes and said, "You're the boss."

The next day Ivy came to pick me up in Long Beach at the port. It is only a two-mile drive from our home. We spent the day together and at four o'clock in the afternoon Ivy dropped me off at the gangway.

I went back to my cabin to find my cabin key would not open the door. I swiped it endlessly and audibly cursed when it would not open. In frustration, I banged on the door with my fist. I stood there for ten minutes knowing that the person who could get me a new key was not in her office and would not be until after we sailed.

Suddenly the door to my cabin opens from the inside! There is a guy who is in my cabin and he locked me out of my cabin where all of my personal possessions were! I did not understand who this was and assumed I was being robbed. I rushed the guy and went for his throat pushing him back in the cabin a good ten feet where he hit the desk.

He started to fight back and said he was a comedian who worked on the ship. I backed off and he explained that each week he was the regular act on the Paradise who used this cabin. He got on the ship today and used his key from previous trips to access my cabin. Carnival Cruise Lines had NEVER changed the key codes on any of the cabins on any of their ships in the fleet. This meant that a key could be used for years to access a cabin! This also applied to passenger cabins.

I was fuming! I could not imagine anyone who would recognize that someone else's personal possessions were strewn about the cabin and to continue staying in that cabin with no hesitation. There was something seriously wrong with this picture.

The comedian kept telling me that I should move my stuff to another cabin. He claimed that this cabin was his and I was going to have to leave.

I looked at the cabin door and said, "See this sign? It says 232. I do not see where it says 'ASSHOLE', now get out of my cabin!"

At this time the scene created enticed others out of their cabins to see what the commotion was. It was me screaming at this asshole!

One little girl who sang in the show said, "It is none of my business but he DOES stay in that cabin each week."

I said, "You are 100% right. It is none of your business!"

She began to scream. She was furious at what I said. She barked, "Ain't no white motherfucker going to tell me to shut up! Not on Christmas Eve!"

Now a really ugly scene is playing out. I have a young girl screaming racist comments. I have an intruder barking at me to move out of his cabin. The Cruise Director thinks I am an anti-Semitic Jew.

The assistant Cruise Director stops by and says, "I do not want to call the Cruise Director on this. Why not just move your stuff out of the cabin?"

I charged into the cabin and packed my bags in about 45 seconds. I grabbed everything and headed to the gangway. I insisted that my passport be handed back to me. The girl at the desk did not know what to do. She picked up the phone and began to dial.

I yelled at her, "You do not need to dial anyone in order to give me my passport! I am an American and we are in an American port and I want off this ship! Now get my fucking passport or I will jump out the cargo door into the water and there will be a huge problem."

She nervously grabbed my passport and I walked off the ship within a few minutes of the ship leaving Long Beach. I called Ivy to meet me at the port and told her that I had just quit. Ivy was there in fifteen minutes to get me.

While in the car back to our place my cell phone rang. It was the Cruise Director! He caught wind of the incident and was begging for me to come back to the ship. I explained that Carnival Cruise Lines and I were no longer a good fit. I went on to say that I was put in jeopardy by Carnival Cruise Lines for the very last time. He begged for me to turn around as the ship was waiting well past sailing time so they could sail with a headliner for the showroom.

I laughed at how this Cruise Director was so sheepish and was now begging me to return to the ship. The night before he was calling me a liar and telling me my material was anti-Semitic! Now he wanted this lying anti Semite Jew to hurry back to the ship!

I said, "You have a comedian who was in my cabin. Have him headline the shows!"

I hung up the phone and never spoke with Carnival Cruise Lines again.

Over the years I had been flown into foreign countries with no information on where to go, how to get there or spent the night in a sub/standard hotel in a dangerous neighborhood in cities I hope to never visit again. I had stayed in cabins where drugs were stashed by other crew members exposing me to charges and potentially prosecution. I was asked to climb cargo nets to board ships while they were moving at high rates of speed endangering me physically. I was exposed to crew members with Hepatitis who lied on their documents when they were hired. I had my passport stolen by a security guard! I witnessed my friend fall through a stage and be permanently handicapped. All of these things and more occurred while I was working for Carnival Cruise Lines.

There were some great people at Carnival Cruise Lines. I have lifelong friends as a result of all my time on Carnival

Cruise Lines ships and for that I am very grateful. I had earned a living and paid my bills and enjoyed a considerable amount of my time when working for Carnival Cruise Lines. To be honest Carnival Cruise Lines enabled me to meet a beautiful woman who I eventually married and I am still married to.

Every Jewish Boy Should Meet the Pope

One of my all time favorite friendships is with my buddy Dougie Pinkerton who I met in Barcelona on Renaissance Cruise Line R2. We met the afternoon I signed on and by the end of the one month contract I was finishing we were great friends.

Dougie was from Scotland but lived in Dubai most of his life and was now living in Portugal. Dougie worked on ships for decades. He had risen through the ranks to Crew Purser. He knew everyone on the ship by name and by face. He could tell what department they worked in and what country they hailed from.

Dougie was also a smoker and could be found in the only smoke friendly location on a Renaissance Cruise Line ship and that was the crew bar. Midori and Seven Up and Rothschild cigarettes were always close by. The regular crowd of smokers would shuffle in and out of the crew bar. There were the waiters and waitresses on break who smoked like vacuums in order to run back to the dining rooms on time. The casino staff were always there and just about 40% of the crew who were smokers. The crew bar was always packed!

The nights were always filled with great people, laughter and booze! Story telling was the best entertainment the crew bar offered. Dougie had some amazing stories to share.

Dougie was living in Scotland and was dating a doctor. In order to fulfill one his fantasies Dougie decided to dress up as Batman. When the doctor got home Dougie surprised him by jumping from the dresser to the bed and dislocated his shoulder. In full Batman regalia, Dougie had to be rushed to the emergency room. While waiting in the ER a little boy was staring at Dougie still dressed as Batman.

The little boy asked Dougie, "What's wrong, Batman?" Dougie was experiencing way too much pain to play along and yelled at the little boy, "Piss off!!!"

The little boy began to cry and scream, "Batman yelled at me! Batman yelled at me!"

My favorite Dougie story was in Rome on a ship's tour of the Vatican. On a ship's tour they hurry you along in a group from one room to another. You see magnificent paintings and amazing sculptures. One room is more impressive than the previous. As they guide you through the Vatican they hurry you along because there is another group trailing right behind. You hardly get a chance to appreciate the value of being in the Vatican.

As the tour is going along and Dougie and I are lagging behind more and more we continue to get chastised by the tour guide. In one room there was a red velvet curtain hanging on what appeared to be a wall. Dougie taps me on the shoulder and points to the spot where the curtains meet. You could just make out a small frail hand as it began to move the curtains. Once the curtains opened it revealed they were the hands of Pope John Paul. He was two feet away from us separated by a velvet curtain and a velvet rope.

The Pope stood there smiling. Dougie, who is Catholic, was giggling with delight and without hesitation said, "Hello your Popeyness!" All that went through my mind was, "Hello your 'Popeyness'? Your 'Popeyness'?" It started to sound correct! Immediately both Dougie and I started to laugh hysterically causing a scene. Two gentleman in blue suits escorted Dougie and I out of the Vatican. We never asked why. We just kept walking until we were back in Rome.

I returned to the Vatican in 2004 with my wife afraid that I might be recognized as "that asshole who called his Holiness 'Your Popeyness'!"

Don't Buy Anyone a Drink

In 2000 technology was booming and cruise ships introduced internet cafés on ships. They charged an outrageous $1.00 per minute for use of computer terminals hooking you up to the web. In order to access the use of the system I had to hook up with the café manager and have my name entered into their billing system. The manager, Zeid, told me to remind him before I signed off the ship to have the charges reversed. All went as planned and Zeid reversed thousands of dollars in charges.

Zeid's contract was over and his replacement was a young Canadian kid named Nigel. This was his first job and first time away from home. He was a fun kid and had a heart of gold. Before I could even explain my deal with Zeid he offered free access to the internet. I was made! For the next three months I would not have to pay for access. In the end the café billed me over $1,400.00 in charges that Nigel reversed.

As a thank you I offered to take Nigel out anywhere he wanted in any port he chose. One night in Athens I returned to the ship at about 8:00 when the ship was doing an overnight. Nigel was hanging out in the port building and suggested that tonight would be a great night to take me up on my offer. I obliged.

We jumped into a taxi and Nigel told the driver to take us a to a strip club. I had never been to a strip club in Greece so I did not think that was a bad idea. Then I realized that the driver was going to take us to a club that he had a connection with. Taxi drivers around the world are notorious for knowing exactly where the action is. Our driver would get a kick back from the club for bringing us to their establishment.

We went inside as the taxi driver was shaking hands with the well dressed man at the door. Obviously he was the guy in charge and the man who paid off the taxi drivers. We sat down at a table and just like any strip club we ordered two Coronas. They were delivered and we paid roughly $15.00 for two beers.

Nigel was so young that I knew this was a first for him. I only gave him one warning and that was, "Do not buy any drinks for any strippers!"

When a stripper sits down at a club she will ask if she can order a drink. What they order is usually water delivered in champagne bottles. Of course it is the most expensive drink on the menu and you have no idea what the price is because there is no price list.

Earlier in the year I witnessed the same scam go down in Hamburg, Germany with the ship's saxophone player. The saxophone player decided to have drinks at a strip club. I tried to discourage this and suggested we go find The Cavern Club where the Beatles played.

We walked into a dingy club on the Reeperbahn at ten in the morning. The bartender rang a bell and six of the ugliest women in Germany appeared from behind a sheet hung from the ceiling. The saxophone player sat down and five of the six girls joined him at his table. The waiter ran to the table and offered him free drinks all day if he bought drinks for the girls.

I felt uncomfortable and awkward and I did not want to be there. I told the saxophone player I was going to walk down the street and wander about for an hour and then I would be back to pick him up.

By the time I got back the saxophone player was sitting in the booth with empty glasses and empty champagne bottles. The girls were giggling and clinging to the saxophone player who was sitting in the booth with his shirt off. The girls were all clothed but the sax player was topless. I thought this picture was priceless.

The bartender rushed to ask what I would like to drink and I asked the sax player how much he spent. He had no idea. I suggested that he ask the bartender what the tab was before going any further. I was sure that he spent a fortune but was not ready for the number the bartender gave him. He had spent over $1,600.00 in a matter of ninety minutes!

He paid the tab. Drank more of the free scotch they offered him and all of the strippers disappeared behind the sheet hanging from the ceiling. He was so drunk upon returning to the ship that he was physically restrained to keep him from fighting the ship's Captain.

Back in the Athens strip club I had to use the bathroom. Before leaving the table I told Nigel, "Do not buy any drinks for any girls."

I come back from the restroom to find two Russian girls sitting with Nigel. Drinks were already delivered to the strippers and Nigel thought he was doing great sitting with two pretty strippers.

I asked Nigel, "Did you not hear me when I said no drinks for strippers?"

Nigel hesitated and then said, "How much could it be? Our drinks were only $15.00."

As the waiter walked by I asked him how much the drinks were. He brought a bill for $300.00!

I yelled at Nigel that this round was on him! Nigel asked that the manager come to the table.

The well dressed man who spoke to our cab driver at the door came to the table. He was the manager. He allowed Nigel to explain to him exactly what happened and why he was not going to pay the bill. This polite gentleman in a suit and American style cowboy boots was very clear to Nigel that the bill had to be paid. Nigel was not having any of that and became very abusive and threatened to leave without paying.

The well dressed Greek man in cowboy boots leaned into the table and said, "This is not America. It is the wild wild west and I am the fucking cowboy in charge!" As he leaned forward you could see his gun in its holster. I was very scared and started to apologize for Nigel's behavior. I explained that he was not very polite and I was embarrassed by his behavior. I knew this guy was not going to be OK with Nigel's plan of walking out.

I said that we needed to go to the ATM on the corner. My plan was to jump into one of the dozens of cabs sitting out in front of the club and take off like a mad man. The manager of the strip club let us go to the ATM. He was watching our every move from the door of the club. We got outside and there were no cabs! Fifteen minutes earlier there was a line around the block and now no cabs!

Nigel ran up to a Greek cop writing tickets to cars parked on the street. Nigel was yelling how we were being ripped off and how he had a gun and how he threatened us but Nigel did not speak Greek and the cops did not speak English. The cop just ignored Nigel! To make matters worse Nigel did this ten feet from the strip club manager who laughed at us.

The manager said, "I own the fucking cops! I told you this was the wild, wild, west and I was the cowboy in charge. Go get my money!"

I feared for my life. Nigel said he did not have access to an ATM and did not have cash on him. I walked over to the ATM and took out the $300.00. I paid the club manager and again apologized for my friend's behavior. Nigel attempted to go back inside as if to finish his beer and to continue talking to the strippers.

The club manager told Nigel, "Your money is no good here. It would be better for your safety if you leave now."

We walked about twenty blocks before finding another taxi back to the ship. Nigel was very quiet in the car. He now owed me $300.00 and he only made $1,200.00 a month. That was a full week's salary. I made a deal with Nigel that he did not have to pay me back. As far as I was concerned I was still saving $1,100 over what I owed for using the internet café.

I did tell Nigel that I had the right to share that story with anyone. I think I just did that.

The Captain's Request

One Captain I had worked with insisted in a very strange way that I tell his favorite cruise ship themed joke every night he was at the show. Prior to my first show, the Captain made me aware that a classic joke about a magician and the ship's Captain made him laugh every time he heard the joke. He insisted that I tell his favorite joke during my show.

I told this joke every night the Captain attended the show. On one particular night I was scheduled to perform the ship was traveling through some rough weather.

In the middle of my show the microphone went dead and over the public address system you could hear the Captain in his broken English, "This is the Captain. This is the Captain addressing you from the ship's bridge. Tonight we are sailing through some areas with high winds. As a safety measure we ask that you do not open your balcony doors. Again this has been your Captain. Bon Voyage."

I could now hear my microphone kick back to live. I said, "How about a hand for your Captain looking out for everyone's safety?!"

Everyone in the showroom applauded.

I then said, "By the way. He isn't really Italian. It is the ship's policy that he pretends to be Italian in order to make

81

your vacation more exciting. He gets an extra $1,000.00 a month to pretend he is Italian. He is really from New Jersey and his name is Bernie Goldstein. When you see the Captain around the ship or in port just say, 'Hello Captain Goldstein!'"

For this I was called into the Captain's cabin and told that I was being fired. I was pretty upset with myself and thought I could talk my way out of being fired. I was sweating this one. I had never been fired and wanted to keep my streak alive. While I was trying to explain myself and save my job I could hear the laughter of others in the Captain's cabin. He had his entire staff hiding behind the curtains listening to him chastise me for being flippant about his name and nationality. It was his way of teaching me a lesson.

That same Captain was let go from the cruise line for crashing into a dock in Malaga, Spain. He had just returned from Tahiti where he had crashed another ship and caused $1,000,000.00 of damage. He was awarded the moniker Captain Crunch.

This was Captain Crunch's favorite joke.

During WWII there was a cruise ship sailing the Mediterranean. Every night the magician performed the ship's Captain would attend the show with his pet parrot on his shoulder.

Each time the magician finished a trick the parrot would yell out, "I know how you did that! I know how you did that!"

This went on for months and the magician despised the parrot. Every night the magician performed he would hear, "I know how you did that! I know how you did that!"

One night the ship was accidentally torpedoed by the German Navy. The ship blew up into a million pieces floating around the Mediterranean. Floating on a piece of wood was the parrot and at the other end was the magician.

For days they floated around with the parrot's eyes deadlocked on the magician's eyes. Finally the parrot says, "OK. I give up. What did you do with the ship?"

Confessions of a Cruise Ship Comedian

This Comedian Needs No Introduction

I boarded the Holiday in San Pedro, California on a Friday afternoon for weekend cruise to Catalina Island and Ensenada, Mexico. I got the cabin key for the cabin which was on a passenger deck near the back of the ship. I knew that the other comedian was in the room next door and eventually I would figure out who it was.

I went about my business and ran into the Cruise Director, Peter. He was a small English man with glasses and a bit of a round figure. He was always sweating and his clothes were ill fitting. He was a sweet and gentle man. Peter told me that the other comedian was Roger and that he had performed his midnight show on Friday after we left San Pedro. Peter said the show was a disaster.

I went about my business without ever seeing Roger. I was going to knock on his door but was not eager to do so. Roger's reputation had preceded him. I had heard that he was an addict and was quite desperate. There was a famous story about Roger breaking into houses while he worked at comedy clubs in cities around the country.

There were stories about missed shows, canceled shows and nights when he was a no show. Roger was a famous topic of comedy club conversation. Sadly in the 1990s Roger spent time in a prison in the Bahamas. He was caught smuggling drugs and had to serve a seven year sentence.

We docked in San Pedro and ended the cruise on Monday morning. I got packed and met Peter, the Cruise Director in the lobby of the ship so that he could walk us through customs. Peter flew into the lobby screaming, "Goodman! Goodman! What in the world did you do to your cabin?! Housekeeping said there was food everywhere! Room service trays piled up and food thrown about!"

I barked back, "Let's go check out the cabin and see what you are talking about." Peter grabbed a key from the Purser's Desk and we headed to the cabin. Peter went to the cabin located next to the one I stayed in. I said, "I did not stay in there. I stayed in the cabin next door." At that moment Peter realized that Roger had stayed in that cabin and was responsible for the mess. He opened the cabin door and found a disaster! I saw dozens of dishes and trays laying everywhere and food all over the floors.

I walked back to the lobby and Peter went to find Roger. With fantastic timing as Peter was leaving Roger arrived in the lobby. He had his bags packed and was ready to sign off. He saw me sitting on the sofa and sat down next to me. Roger introduced himself and said he got himself in trouble on this cruise.

I did not say a word about having seen his cabin and I played it dumb! Roger went on to tell me he had a bad show Friday night and to cheer himself up he went gambling in the casino. This was a major violation of the rules. I knew that Carnival Cruise Lines would fire him without hesitation and I think Roger knew that. Roger went on tell me that he used his bank debit card and got a $500.00 advance even though his account balance was zero. This story was getting better and better.

Roger also admitted that he was questioned by security over an incident in the casino. Roger said that a player at the craps table accused Roger of stealing his chips. The accusation led to security and casino management reviewing the video cameras. Roger said the video clearly shows that he stole the chips and he feared arrest. To boot Roger told me that he was smuggling 15 cartons of untaxed cigarettes off the ship.

I was astonished that anyone could do so much damage in a matter of a few days. I was scared for him!

In the hallway off the lobby I could hear Peter's little shuffle as he dragged his feet across the carpet. I felt like I wanted to be invisible and did not want to witness Peter losing his cool with Roger. I feared that Roger might knock Peter out.

Peter angrily pointed at Roger and yelled, "What the fuck did you do?"

Peter looked over at me and said, "Goodman get off the ship and tell customs I will be right down."

I grabbed my bags and headed off the ship.

I never heard what happened to Roger for his actions on the Holiday. I know he never worked for Carnival Cruise Lines again.

A few years ago I heard that Roger had overdosed on Ambien.

The Millennium is Special

The Millennium was a great marketing plan for the cruise lines. They were hiring high end celebrities on every ship. They were offering all kinds of free swag like back packs, rolling luggage, bathrobes, Pierre Jouet champagne and more. Of course everything was emblazoned with the Carnival Cruise Lines logo.

I was told by the entertainment office that the money for the trip was being bumped up considerably. Carnival Cruise Lines was also allowing us to bring a companion-at Carnival Cruise Lines's expense!

I did not know who to call. I was not dating anyone and did not have any prospects. I thought about asking my buddy Mark but he was planning on spending New Year's Eve with his girlfriend.

I then thought about calling my high school friend Julie who was living in Phoenix. We once agreed that if we were 40 and not married that we would marry each other so we would not look pathetic. I think I agreed to it and Julie never really committed one way or the other.

I got Julie on the phone and she told me it was not possible to meet me in Acapulco since she would be just returning home from Paris.

The next day Julie called me back and said that her mother told her she was nuts for not going and she changed her mind. She would take me up on my offer and fly home to Phoenix in time to make it to Acapulco on December 31st.

When I called the entertainment office and gave them Julie's information explaining that Julie was first flying in from Paris they suggested they could fly her from Paris to Acapulco. That was perfect and I told Julie about the plan. I was now really looking forward to the Millennium cruise.

I flew on December 30th from Los Angeles to Acapulco via Mexico City. I hate flying through Mexico City. The airport is large, crowded and chaotic. You can easily get caught in long lines at the immigration desk and then wind up missing your flight. This became the routine so much so that the cruise lines would fly the entertainers to the same city on different flights trying to increase the odds that one or more of the acts would make it to the ship.

Travel on this holiday was expected to be outrageous. Add in the fact that the Millennium was great marketing for a rare event to the looming Y2K disaster and it did make for rough travels! I got to LAX early to find my Alaska Airlines flight was canceled.

Instead of negotiating with an Alaska agent for a ticket later in the day or on another carrier I walked over to Mexicana Airlines ticket counter. There was no one in line. I walked right up to the counter. I explained that I needed to get to Acapulco to catch a cruise for Carnival Cruise Lines. The agent checked my ticket and said she could help me out no problems.

Five minutes later she printed my ticket and issued me a first class seat! I loved Mexicana Airlines. They had direct flights to Acapulco but this diversion was also via Mexico City.

I got through the airport in Mexico City quickly. I even rode the elevator with Ben Vereen who was heading to a Royal Caribbean ship along with Alan King who was heading to a different Carnival Cruise Lines ship for Millennium shows.

I landed in Acapulco close to sunset and jumped into a cab. This was not the usual small VW Bug that is best at handling the tight curves of the road from the airport. I was in a huge 1970's era Ford Torino station wagon. One just like my Dad drove when I was a kid. It was the SUV of its day and not the best car for a tight road with lots of tight turns.

Thankfully traffic was so busy for the Millennium holiday that we had no choice but to drive slowly all the way to the hotel. Well, I thought it was a hotel when I read my itinerary.

As we were driving to the hotel resort Las Hamacas you could see how beautiful a city Acapulco is. The main avenue from the airport is lined with lush green landscaped hotels, cliffs, blue ocean vistas, and million dollar homes. Further down is the port and you can see cruise ships anchored off the bay.

As we crept along the main avenue it was lined with beaches on one side and businesses on the other. I looked out the window to find my buddy Denny, a singer who also worked for Carnival Cruise Lines, walking right next to the cab. I told the driver to stop and asked Denny where the hotel was. Denny gracefully waved his arms like a magician revealing the empty cage once occupied by a tiger and pointed to the building behind him.

Las Hamacas was a dump! I found out that in Spanish Las Hamacas means the hammocks! The cab driver helped me with my bag and waved good-bye as my stomach sank. Denny was telling me how bad the rooms were when I got to the desk and rang the bell for help. Denny told me we had no choice but to spend the night. He said that all the hotels had been sold out for the Millennium or have a three night minimum.

I got a key to my room and took the elevator up to the top floor. I opened the door and Denny jumped in front of me to look around the room. I was in shock. It was a flea bag motel and not a hotel resort as my paperwork from the office said it was.

Denny looked at me and said, "This place is great compared to my room!"

I could not imagine how bad his room was and I did not want to see it! I told Denny I could not spend the night and he repeated himself that no rooms were available. We agreed we would spend the night out having dinner as late as possible to avoid having to be in the roach motel.

We walked over to the Krazy Lobster. It was on the beach next to the bungee jumping rig which was a big tourist attraction.

We got there early enough to score a coveted table on the deck with great views of the bungee jumping and the waves hitting the beach. The waiter took our order without mentioning that it was happy hour. He returned with 6 shots of Cuervo Tequila and 6 Coronas in an ice bucket. I love happy hour!

Technically, we were traveling on company business and the company covered all of our travel related expenses including meals. This was about to be an epic meal. Denny and I had both been to the Krazy Lobster before and its reputation as a party locale was legendary.

We ate, drank and smoked from about 7:30 to midnight. We dined on lobster, shrimp and everything they brought to the table. We drank more beer and devoured more Cuervo. We were hammered and sticking to the plan that we were not going back to the hotel.

Denny came up with our next move and told me we were on our way to a strip club he had been to before.

We jumped out of the taxi and headed to stand in the velvet roped line at the front door.

As we walk to the velvet rope I hear, "Dave Goodman! Mr. Goodman! What are you doing here?!"

I looked over at this guy in a poor fitting suit who started reciting jokes from my act almost verbatim. He rushed over to us and shook my hand. He escorted us right into the club to a booth in front of the main stage. He said he would send over the first round.

I remembered who he was. He was a porter at the Riviera Hotel and Casino in Las Vegas when I lived there. I think his name was Manny and he ferried ice from the freezers to the various bars in the casino. He would deliver ice to the showroom bar.

We stayed at the club until about 4:00 AM. I remember a lot of dancers coming to our table and a lot of pictures being taken. I remember everything clearly up until this point in time. This is when my memory starts to get a little fuzzy.

Denny announced that he knew the best place to go for breakfast and into another taxi we went. We navigated the hills and stopped in front a huge white mansion in a really quiet neighborhood.

We walked up to the gate and a young kid dressed in white ran down some stairs and let us in. We walked up the stairs to a fantastic view of Acapulco and an amazing outdoor patio and bar.

There were a few people mingling at the bar and swimming in a pool.

Denny plopped down on a sofa and barked out, "I only have a hundred dollars and all I want is a massage."

A few seconds later a procession of girls in bathing suits and negligees line up right in front of the sofa.

A man who looked like an ad for a cigar company said, "Señor, please choose any girl." Denny again says, "All I want is a massage."

Now I knew exactly where we were!

Denny grabbed a girl and went up the stairs and inside the mansion. I waited by the bar while every girl in the brothel hit on me. I was feeling really uncomfortable and did not know how long I could handle this.

Suddenly I hear the door from the garden open and walking down the stairs is Denny.

I looked up at the door and Denny said, "That was the best massage I ever had!"

I looked at my watch and I think seven minutes had passed since Denny first left for his massage. It was the best seven minute massage of his life.

Denny grabbed a beer and we stayed at the brothel until the sun came up. We jumped into a taxi and went back to Las Hamacas with intentions of grabbing our bags and heading to the port to wait for the Holiday to dock.

I was never so glad to not spend the night in such a horrible place. I think had I spent the night it would have damaged me for the rest of my life.

We got to the ship at 7:30 AM. We got cabin keys and said goodnight. I was expecting Julie at some point in the day and thought to myself staying in the cabin was a good idea.

At about 2:00 I got up and wandered into the port. I sat down at the bar and ordered a Diet Coke. I was keeping an eye to the entrance expecting Julie to walk through any minute. At 6:00 PM there was no Julie and I did not know what to think. The ship was sailing at 7:00.

I found Julie asleep in my cabin! We somehow crossed paths in the port and she had been napping since 3:00. We got dressed and headed out for a night of crazy drinking and partying. We were on the lido deck at midnight when the Captain began lighting fireworks from the top deck of the ship.

The passengers were downing booze by the bottle as they were being passed from person to person. Kids were running around shouting and drunk women were kissing any man standing near them.

Julie and I called it quits and we were probably in bed by 1:00 AM. We were such party animals. I was actually trying to recover from the night before and I had to perform the next night.

Julie and I got up for breakfast and left the cabin. We headed to the buffet on the Lido Deck. It was now cleared of empty glass, empty bottles, confetti and other trash.

We grabbed a table with our dishes in hand. It was 9:00 in the morning and we were the only people having breakfast. There were various sightings of others but most everyone was still passed out. I went to the bar for orange juice and coffee.

There was only one passenger in front of me talking to the bartender.

The passenger turned around quickly and said, "Good morning. Happy New Year!"

I asked, "Why are you not hung over?"

She laughed and told me she was not a drinker and then asked why I was not hung over. I explained I was nursing a two day hang over. She asked what I was doing on the ship and I barely remember giving her an answer before I started to notice her beautiful smile and how tall she was and her red hair.

I grabbed my coffee and headed back to Julie.

Julie said, "Who were you talking to? Why are you not still talking to her? You better go find her and talk to her!"

I laughed it off until Julie and I were in port in the lovely and quiet town of Zihuatanejo, Mexico. Zihuatanejo is the magical city where Andy Dufresne disappeared to in *The Shawshank Redemption*. It was New Year's Day and everything in town was closed except for an ice cream shop. Julie and I stopped by and got a couple of scoops.

We sat down in the town square and in the distance you could see the young lady I spoke to earlier that morning. I told Julie that was her. We sat there debating if it was indeed the same girl. I was skeptical and decided not to say anything. As she got closer and closer I was less and less convinced if it was the same girl. I decided to not say anything.

We got back to the ship and had dinner. Julie was so tired that she wanted to go to bed and at 10:00 I decided to set out to find the girl from the Lido Deck bar.

At about 10:30 I hear a young lady's voice and turned to see the girl from the Lido Deck bar! We introduced ourselves to each other. Her name was Phyllis but preferred Ivy. She was on the ship with a group of people from work. She asked why I did not say hello in Zihuatanejo. I told her that Julie and I had talked about whether it was or was not her.

Ivy said, "Your girlfriend is cute."

I answered very quickly, "We're not dating. We are just best friends since high school."

Ivy seemed very happy to hear that explanation.

We walked around the ship for hours. We played ping pong on deck and sat in the library talking until 4:30 in the morning.

I walked Ivy back to her cabin and said good night.

The next night was my show. That afternoon we were going to be in Manzanillo, Mexico. Denny had made plans to have lunch with Shirley Jones, who was also performing on the Holiday, and her musical director at Las Hadas Resort. This is the same resort that the movie "10" was shot at. The scene of Bo Derek running on the beach is right behind the hotel. Denny told me to tag along and I mentioned that I had Julie with me and that I met a passenger. He said to bring them all along.

So my first date with Ivy was with my best friend Julie and Shirley Jones from the Partridge Family and her son and heart throb Shaun Cassidy. There were others along but I do not remember who.

What I do remember was talking to Ivy and thinking about seeing her again! She was quiet and polite but could participate in a conversation with her sweet disposition and her easy laugh. We walked on the beach and talked about seeing each other in Los Angeles. She was living in Cypress which was about a 40 mile drive to my place in Venice.

At one point Shirley got into a pedal boat and was getting caught in the tide. Someone swam to her rescue while we watched from a rock on the beach. At that moment I assured Ivy I was going to see her again in Los Angeles.

I did my shows that night and had to pack to head back to Los Angeles from Puerto Vallarta, Mexico. Ivy was still vacationing on the ship all the way back to San Pedro. It would be another four days for her before reaching home.

The morning before Julie and I left for the airport we went to lunch with Ivy. We took pictures at the beach and hugged goodbye. I was confident I would see her again.

The ship returned to San Pedro on Friday. It was running four hours late into port. I had to catch a flight to Las Vegas but wanted to meet the ship and see Ivy as she got off. I thought it would give her great confidence to see that I met her that morning to say hello.

While killing time waiting for the ship I noticed a little blonde haired woman. She was also waiting for the ship. She wandered about for a while and even seemed to eavesdrop on my phone conversation.

The ship arrived and the doors opened. Ivy was one of the first passengers to clear customs and get off the ship. I was standing there smiling. Ivy got through the doors and she was wearing a huge smile. Her arms were outstretched ready for a hug. She made a beeline for the little blonde woman I had noticed in the port.

It dawned on me that this must be Ivy's mom. While hugging her mom Ivy looked over her shoulder and saw me standing there. She ran over to say "hello" and gave me a great big hug. I told her I had to rush to the airport but wanted to say "hello" and see her again. Her mother followed Ivy over. Ivy awkwardly introduced her mother to me. She was very confused as to why I was already off the ship and in port waiting for the ship if Ivy said we met on the ship.

Ivy said she would explain it all to her mother later at home. I ran off to the airport for my Las Vegas shows.

We have been together ever since.

Keep Your Jokes to Yourself

My first Carnival Cruise Lines trip was out of San Pedro, California. I was home on a Saturday night when my phone rang. It was an agent out of South Florida who offered me a trip on the Elation to fill in for an act who got sick.

I was living in West Los Angeles and my roommate dropped me off at the ship. I checked in and got a quick education in learning how to fend for myself. There was no one available to answer any questions. To my advantage my good friend Lowell was also sailing on this cruise. I knew that Lowell would show me the ropes.

The night we left San Pedro I had two shows in the main showroom. After the first show the orchestra and Cruise Director funneled down the stairs behind the stage to the crew bar. Lowell was there and I followed him to the crew bar.

The show went well and it was certainly a different kind of show than I was familiar with. There were children everywhere. Kids do not process comedy like adults do and are therefore terrible audiences for comedians. Adults were still settling in and wandering in and out of the theater. There were lots of distractions to learn to deal with but the show went OK.

I was sweating and needed a drink. I got a Diet Coke and went back to the tables taken over by the orchestra and Lowell. The entire orchestra was on edge and acting odd. Finally the musical director, Joe, leaned forward and as if he was speaking for the entire orchestra and asked, "Why are you doing Mick Lazinski's act?"

Mick was also a comedian who worked on the Elation for Carnival Cruise Lines. Mick and I met in Albuquerque 12 years earlier and were friends. I had even booked Mick into Las Vegas for more money than he ever made before! That week in Vegas Mick kept thanking me and telling me he would do anything to help me in return for his Las Vegas bookings.

Mick, Lowell and I were all friends. We had worked on the road together for years. When I was booking a show in Las Vegas, Lowell and Mick were my first bookings.

Here I was being questioned about stealing my material. I was shocked! Mick was supposedly my friend. Why would he be telling my jokes? Why would the orchestra's musical director approach me like I was a thief who got caught stealing their friend's jokes?

Lowell started to laugh and said, "Now I know why Mick never wanted you working on this ship. It's because he is doing your act out here!"

Joe kept repeating lines from my act referring to specific jokes. Joe said, "Bargain Hunter" and I answered, "My joke." Joe would say, "Covered in Chocolate" and I answered, "My joke."

If Lowell were not there to confirm this I would have been branded a thief by the orchestra.

Joe and the rest of the orchestra laughed and realized that Mick was a bit of a dodgy character. They had given him way too much credit. They were developing a plan to embarrass Mick about this. I did not discourage them.

I got back home and phoned Mick. I was really mad. Here is my friend using my jokes to pay his bills. That was something I was not OK with. Mick did not answer his phone. I found out that Joe had called him from the port and blasted him for thievery. Lowell also did the same on a few occasions when they were on the ship together.

Mick eventually called me to apologize. He said that he was sorry and never thought he would get caught. He went on to say that he would never do the jokes again. He tried to justify his thieving but conceded he was wrong and sorry for it.

Two years later my wife went on a family cruise on the Elation out of San Pedro. I was working and did not take part in the cruise. The comedian on the ship was Mick

Lazinski. My wife was shocked to hear my material coming from his mouth. It is proof that in comedy you cannot trust anyone who steals material.

I have not spoken to Mick in years. He got divorced after his wife found out he was lying to her. Carnival Cruise Lines would no longer hire him after years of corrupt behavior. He no longer lives in Los Angeles and moved out of state.

Meeting New People

There are several types of cruises that you might not be aware of. The corporate office might sell a voyage to a specific group at a discounted rate. The groups range from ethnic cruises for Indians and Persians all the way to lifestyle choices like nude cruises or even themed cruises that cater to the gay community. The entertainment office is not always aware of these bookings.

I personally have been on ships where there were 1,500 non-English speaking Indians. Have you ever attempted to have a conversation with someone who does not speak English? Now imagine having a conversation with 1,500 non-English speaking people! Imagine that conversation has to last for 45 minutes and you have to do all of the talking! Now add in the absurd idea that you are supposed to be entertaining and making non-English speaking people laugh.

I stood there amongst a sea of smiling and confused people. They wanted to see big Bollywood type dance numbers and here I am in my suit asking, "Did anyone else here tonight go to Hebrew School?"

I got off the stage furious that I had to do the show. I yelled at the Cruise Director that he was feeding me to the sharks. He told me that he had no choice and that Miami (meaning the office) did not allow for the right kind of entertainment.

He told me that this problem had been going on all week. Then he promises me, "The second show will go much better!"

There were cruises for nudists. I got on the ship and thought they were shooting Candid Camera. I was walking to my cabin in the crew area of the ship and was taking the elevator down. The doors opened up and twenty naked people crammed into the elevator! I touched an ass and to this day I am not certain it was a female ass.

Theme Cruises

On a gay cruise in Mexico I finished my shows and headed to the casino bar to meet up with my friend Denny. Denny was in his early fifties with a full head of mostly salt and pepper hair and he worked out regularly. He was a good looking guy but he always struck out when hitting on girls half his age.

Denny was smiling from ear to ear about the craziness of the cruise. He was a veteran of lots of gay cruises and was very comfortable hanging out. We were sitting at the bar when two guys came over to chat with us. We assumed they saw the shows.

They were flamboyant and way over the top. Denny was being manhandled by one of the guys. He was stroking Denny's hair and ran his finger up and down his chest. I was laughing at how uncomfortable Denny was. Finally this guy says, "Hey! Let's go back to our cabin and all of us can make each other happy, if you know what I mean?!"

Denny said, "I know exactly what you mean!" Denny took off walking at a really fast pace so he would not upset the gentleman who made the offer. There I was with these two guys. They turned their attentions to me and I had to duck out while keeping my dignity.

I turned to say good night and slipped on the floors that were just being mopped. I wiped out like a cartoon flat on my back! These two guys come running over to help.

They got me back on my feet and made sure I was OK. Once again they made me the same offer they made to Denny with the added bonus of a massage for my aching back.

Before Viagra

On a Princess Cruise Line cruise I met a gentleman who was 85. He was celebrating what would have been his 60th wedding anniversary had his wife not passed away. He explained that they loved cruising and had taken over 40 cruises while they were together.

He told me that he had this cruise planned prior to his wife's death and decided he would take the cruise in her memory. He even brought along a date. He told me he was traveling with a woman and that he was in the dog house.

He explained to me that he had missed his wife very much but needed companionship not sex. He freely shared that his 'machinery' was missing some parts and could not do any of the heavy lifting.

He had invited a woman who he and his wife knew to go on the cruise. She was staying in her own cabin. He felt like there was a connection and that there might be a rendezvous for the two of them on this cruise. He came prepared. He had visited his doctor who gave him a syringe to inject into his penis in the off chance there might be some love making. This was way before Viagra and Cialis.

He told me the night was great. They dined together and after dinner they danced in the lounge for hours. Thinking he was getting lucky he excused himself to his cabin where he injected his penis with the syringe from his doctor.

He went back to the lounge to find his lady friend. She was tired and wanted to go to bed. He was reading the signals and realized he was about to get lucky. When they got to her cabin she said good night and closed the door. He misread the signals!

Now this poor old man had a chemically induced erection and had no one to share it with. However, he was completely comfortable telling me about it!

I said, "Well there isn't anything I can do to help you either."

I said, "Good night," and went to my cabin.

I saw this same guy twice the next day and sure enough his chemically induced erection was still in full spirits! You couldn't miss it!

Really Great People

Some of the brightest and most intelligent people I have met have worked at cruise lines.

I knew a Maitre D at Renaissance Cruise Line who was from Lithuania. He was sweet and kind and a trained doctor. He practiced medicine in Lithuania for the government and could only make the equivalent of $900.00 (American dollars) per month. As a Maitre D he was making about $2,800.00 a month plus tips.

After working a few contracts he expected to be able to buy a house for his parents and another for his family and still be able to go back to being a doctor. He was also the best musician on the ship! He could play the piano and loved the classics of Bach and Beethoven. He would play without charts and according to other musicians he never missed a note!

Many of the wait staff spoke three and four languages. Some had been school teachers, lawyers, accountants, chefs, bank managers, Hotel Managers, and more.

They all had a few things in common and that was making money, traveling and living life like an adventure.

They worked very hard. Some worked eighteen hour days, seven days a week for eight or nine months with an occasional day off. Others had easier hours or less physical obligations. Your pay was based on what department you worked in and what country you hailed from.

There was an Austrian girl, Inga who was in charge of Food and Beverage. She was much despised by her crew but very respected by management. She ran such a tight department that she had the highest bonuses at Renaissance Cruise Line. She was a tough lady and even though she was attractive she gave the vibe that she was more Frau Blucher from *Young Frankenstein.*

I was forever speaking with Inga as she escaped to the crew bar to smoke throughout the day. I would be there with my laptop and smokes. She was fun and stern and loved her reputation as a bitch.

We would sit in the crew bar and watch *The Sopranos.* I was a huge fan and recorded the shows at home. I even had my girlfriend recording the episodes I missed while out of town. I brought the tapes with me to the R2. The Broadcast Manager, Casey, who was in charge of the ship's entertainment systems including all of the television shows and movies that crew and passengers watched. There was a dedicated crew channel that only the crew could access. Casey played *The Sopranos* on a loop for 24 hours for the entire first season. The crew members were mesmerized by the show and everyone was talking about it.

Inga turned to me one day and said, "I have a filthy mouth but the way these people talk in this show is amazing! 'Fuck this. Fuck that. Fuck you. Fuck me. Get the fuck out of here' Does everyone in New Jersey talk like this?"

We laughed as the TV played out a scene proving Inga's point.

I looked at her and said, "Get the fuck outta here!'

Inga answered, "No. You get the fuck outta here!"

For the remainder of the day we kept that up and it was our own little personal joke.

The next week the ship was embarking new passengers. Inga was part of the crew that lined up with white gloves and white jackets as the new passengers would arrive. It was very formal and very dignified.

As Inga stood in line I sneaked up on her and whispered in her ear, "Get the fuck outta here!"

She loudly and clearly responded, "You get the fuck outta here!"

Inga then realized where she was and ran away in horror!

The passengers were not really sure what to make of it.

These were the kinds of moments that I loved about being on the ship. Having fun was my mission every day. I had way too much down time between shows and I entertained myself with laughter.

I became friendly with anyone and everyone. I wanted to be considered a nice guy and I think I accomplished that.

The officers were very accessible on Renaissance Cruise Line. They were very nice guys who treated me with great respect. I know some of them well enough that I still get Christmas cards every year.

I have my Nepalese friends, Jit Ranna in particular, who think I am moving to Katmandu. I once told them I wanted to move there and be known as the Katmandu Jew. They never really got the joke.

There are still a dozen or so friendships created at sea that I still spend time with to this day. Some of these friends have spent weeks visiting my wife and I at home in California. Some I get to visit while I travel around the country.

Don't I Know You?

My wife, Ivy, and I were at the airport in Detroit changing planes. A guy was sitting across from me staring at me and not trying to hide it. He eventually walked over and asked, "Are you the comedian from the R5?" I recognized him from Renaissance Cruise Line. His name was Romeo and he was a Philippine Bosun. He was traveling to another ship in Houston, Texas. He hugged me like we were best friends.

The chances of running into someone you know in a locale far from your home is really slim. I have seemed to overcome those slim odds.

I had worked in Europe with a great musician and true gentleman from New Orleans. His name is Rick Hardeman. Rick was working the same run from Barcelona to Italy for a month before I got to the ship. Rick was in his early 50s and had very little in common with the crew members. He rarely ever stepped into the crew bar.

After that trip I did not see Rick for ten years. He was not very good at email and keeping in touch. Rick told me that he lived in Hell's Kitchen section of New York City. When Ivy and would visit New York I would walk up 9th or 10th Avenue and I would say, "Rick lives in this neighborhood."

In 2011, I was eating breakfast with Ivy on 7th Avenue right across from our hotel near Central Park. I was looking out

117

the window and there was Rick Hardeman walking by the café! I ran outside and yelled to him. He turned around and immediately knew who was yelling at him on the streets of New York.

We sat and talked for a bit before he had to run to his appointment at the studio next door. The next morning we again saw Rick walk by that same window. I called out to him and had coffee.

The Greatest Cruise Ship Comedian Story

There was one legendary story about working ships that every comedian had heard. As the rumor was started it became common belief that if you performed on a cruise and did not do well they would have you disembark the ship in the next port. It was then up to you to book your own flight back home. No one wanted to risk having to confirm or deny this rumor so for years young comedians did not work on ships.

For years I had heard the fable of Peter Fogel being fired from a cruise line. Peter was working for a ship out of Europe just after the Achille Lauro incident of 1985.

The Achille Lauro was hijacked by four gunmen representing a Palestinian linked terror organization. They held the passengers hostage and eventually took the life of a passenger name Leon Klinghoffer. After his murder he was dumped over the side of the ship in the Mediterranean Sea off Syria. The story was of international interest as an entire ship was being held hostage.

Peter was not on the Achille Lauro. As the story is told, Peter was onstage in the main showroom and was not doing well with the crowd. He was indeed bombing. As comedians will do when things go bad Peter begins to improvise lines and throws out this gem, "Don't forget to try

119

the Klinghoffer at the bar. It's two shots and they dump you over board."

The crowd begins to boo and moan. They grow angrier and angrier. The light and tech crews get a cue from the Cruise Director to cut off his microphone and bring down the curtains.

The Cruise Director, Hotel Manager and the ship's Captain all confronted Peter backstage about his inappropriate reference to Klinghoffer.

Peter was doomed to be fired. He so angered the passengers that the ship did not wait to dock in port to have him leave. Instead they had Peter flown off the ship by helicopter never to be seen again on a cruise ship.

The Truth is I saved His Life!

In 1996 I had the chance to work with Peter at the Improv in Las Vegas. The only reference I ever heard about Peter was the famous cruise ship story. I could not wait to ask him if it were true.

Peter was furious that I asked him. He angrily denied that there was any truth to the story and did not know how the story gained steam.

On Sunday night of our week in Las Vegas I wound up saving Peter's life. We were dining at the Rikshaw in the Riviera Hotel. We were using the last of our room comps before the week was over.

Peter was telling me a story while he was having his won ton soup. He grabbed his glass of water and attempted to have a drink. The water came right out the side of his mouth. He suddenly looked anxious and frightened. He was choking on a won ton.

I jumped up and started the Heimlich maneuver. Peter shot a won ton out of his mouth a good ten feet. People dining at the table next to us started to applaud. The waiter told me, "You are a hero! You saved your buddies' life!"

Things calmed back down and Peter asked me to never tell anyone what just happened. I never gave anyone the

Heimlich in my life and there is no way that I am keeping this story to myself.

We went back to the showroom for our last show. The guy in charge at the time was Steve Schirippa. He was the maitre d and head ball buster. Steve went on to have a very successful career as an actor and is best known as Bobby Bacala from The Sopranos.

The second I saw Steve I could not wait to tell him what just happened.

As we approached the podium in front of the showroom from the escalator I yelled out, "Steve! Ask Peter about how I saved his life!"

As we stepped off the escalator Peter turned and went right back down the escalator.

I filled Steve in on what happened at dinner. Peter eventually returned and Steve spent the rest of the evening ripping Peter apart.

He started with, "Peter Fogel we have your life boat ready! It's stocked with lots of won ton!"

"Hey Peter! How does it feel to have a man grab you from behind like that? Oh yeah, I forgot you already knew how that felt!"

"Hey Peter! Try the Peter Fogel! Its two won tons and a reach around!"

Confessions of a Cruise Ship Comedian

Hecklers are Not Normal

Over the years I have had my share of hecklers. I am proud to say that I have never been on the losing end of a conversation with a heckler. My advantages are numerous. I am not drunk. I have been heckled before. I have a microphone. I have a skill at handling assholes.

On a cruise on the R2 in Europe I was stopped mid-show by a female who was more inquisitive than heckler. She very loudly asked in a theater with 700 passengers, "Where in New York are you from?" Her New York accent had others giggling.

I turned the tables and asked, "Where in New York are YOU from?"

She answered, "Bellmore."

I said, "I'm from Bellmore! What street did you live on?" She yelled, "Judith Drive!"

I knew Judith Drive. I had loads of friends who lived on Judith Drive. It was in my neighborhood and I knew this woman must be from Bellmore.

I went on to ask, "What is your last name?" In a great Brooklyn accent I heard, "Gerstman!" I literally laughed out loud and said nothing for a good 90 seconds.

I took my time. The audience was already laughing at this absurd outbreak in the middle of my show. I was relishing the moment.

Waiting for the perfect time to ask, "How are Michael and Andrew doing?"

The man seated next to her, obviously Mr. Gerstman, jumped to his feet and shouted, "How the hell do you know my kid's names?"

The showroom broke out into huge applause, laughter and sheer craziness.

This man remained standing and again yelled, "How do you know my kids?"

I said, "You do not remember me? I grew up in Bellmore on Lee Place. I was in your house a hundred times! You fed me green bell peppers! You drove me to Hebrew school in your red Lincoln with the white vinyl top!"

Mr. Gerstman yelled out, "How did you know I had a red Lincoln?"

The crowd continued to applaud, laugh and wonder what the hell was going on. Things calmed down a little bit and I asked the Gerstmans how Andrew, my friend, was doing. They were still very unsure of what had transpired and how

I knew who they were. In the darkness of the showroom I heard this, "How the hell does he know who we are?!"

Again the room breaks out into laughter. Mrs. Gerstman now stands and asks, "Are you really from Bellmore?"

I could not resist and over the microphone I said, "No. This was the mind reading portion of my show."

The audience laughed with a little bit of applause and confusion.

Mrs. Gerstman sat back down and you could hear her say, "He's pretty good at it."

That night the Cruise Director brought Mr. and Mrs. Gerstman backstage. Their memories were getting a little clearer and I started to mention all of the names of the guys we grew up with together in Bellmore. Mrs. Gerstman heard me mention about a dozen names before she started to believe my story.

As the cruise continued the Gerstmans became my shadow. They wanted to go everywhere together. They wanted to dine together, have drinks in their cabin together and chat about Bellmore.

What they really loved was the fact that on that particular cruise people were running up to them asking, "Was that real or rehearsed? Do you travel with the comedian every week? How long have you done this act together?" They were pseudo celebrities for the two week cruise.

Don't Piss-Off the Captain's Wife

Crew members all live in the same areas of the ship. They are located in restricted areas that the passengers rarely ever see. The cabins are traditionally booked two to a cabin and the cabin mates are traditionally from the same department on the ship.

These cabins are used for showering, changing clothes, sleep and sex. Not always in that order.

Officers have their own cabins in a different area of the ship. They are generally larger and more accommodating than crew cabins.

There is a tolerance on ships that does not exist in a conventional society. On a ship a married man or woman will often find the comfort of another for the length of their contract. Some relations are very open and some are very much a secret.

There was a Greek ship's Captain who was sleeping with a Hotel Manager. Their relationship was well known and dated back many years. The Captain was rarely ever seen outside of his professional responsibilities. He spent most his time in his cabin. I was on the ship for several months and saw the Captain maybe four times.

The Hotel Manager was from South Africa and quite odd. She was ruthless in her treatment of the crew. She was rude, dismissive and had a history of questionable behavior. She was working on a ship when there was a theft of tens of thousands of dollars from the cache of tips the housekeeping staff received. She was able to save her job and all fingers pointed to her boyfriend, the Captain, as being the one who kept her from losing her job. I heard this story from the person who caught her stealing the money.

The Captain's wife was sailing with the Captain for a week. This was a problem for the Hotel Manager who did not want to come face to face with her lover's spouse. There were several close calls where they almost did meet face to face.

The gentleman who told me about the theft was also a crew member at this time on this cruise. He was aware of the affair and was not at all OK with turning a blind eye to the situation.

The Captain's wife was wandering the decks looking for her husband. He was nowhere to be found. The gentleman who knew the intimate details of the Hotel Manager's past was aware that the Captain was in the cabin of his mistress, the Hotel Manager. When he crossed paths with the Captain's wife he very freely told her that the Captain could be found in cabin 345 next door to the Captain's cabin. The Captain's wife went to cabin 345 and knocked on the door. The Hotel Manager answered the door in a towel and over her shoulder in bed was the Captain. He jumped to his feet naked and caught in the act.

The Captain's wife very calmly packed her bags and readied herself to disembark the ship. As the ship was about to pull up the gangway, she very dramatically cursed at him in Greek, slapped his cheek and yelled in English, "By the time you get home there will be nothing left for you!" She then pulled out a small prescription bottle and unscrewed the cap. She dumped the contents of the prescription into the Aegean Sea. Standing on the gangway she yelled, "Try to fuck your girlfriend now without Viagra!"

Lost Luggage

I flew from Los Angeles to Barcelona, Spain on Lufthansa Airlines. I was going to be gone for four months on a repositioning cruise to the Baltic countries from the Mediterranean Sea. I had packed two very large pieces of luggage. One had all of my clothes I wear for the shows and the other bag had all of my casual stuff.

I landed in Barcelona and collected only one bag at the luggage carousel. It was my garment bag containing all of my clothes for the shows. It had four suits, eight shirts and two pairs of shoes. All of my toiletries and underwear, shorts, t-shirts, socks, and more were in the bag that did not arrive.

I filed a report in Barcelona and headed to my hotel on Las Ramblas, the most famous street in Barcelona. I checked in and headed to my room. I was so stressed out about my bag making it to Barcelona that I stayed up all night pacing Las Ramblas and annoying the front desk clerk if the airlines had delivered anything to my room.

If the bag did not arrive in Barcelona it was going to be a game of cat and mouse to catch up with my bag. I was going to be in a different city everyday for the next four months. How in the hell are they going to catch up with me?

When morning came and I still did not have my bag the reality of having to leave Barcelona without my luggage was overwhelming.

Where am I going to buy underwear, shorts, t-shirts and a few other items in my size in Barcelona? Is there a Spanish big and tall store nearby? Grande y Alto Tienda?!

I walked over to El Corte Ingles. It is the Spanish version of Macys. I went to the men's department and found a new obstacle to getting clothes. The metric system! All of the sizes were in numbers as opposed to letters and the numbers were not something I recognized.

I found only one pair of underwear. I guess between the pair I am wearing and a new pair I could wash them every night and have a fresh pair each day. I bought socks. Socks and underwear! That is all I need. I thought I'll get my bag soon and everything will work out.

I purchased toiletries and headed to the ship. I spoke to the Cruise Director, Crew Purser, Hotel Manager and anyone who would listen to ask for help in looking out for my bag.

I took a shower and planned on changing into some fresh clothes. I opened the package of underwear and put them on. They were quite unusual. They were cut more like a Speedo bathing suit than underwear. I was literally having my package squeezed in a very bad way. From my experience with Spanish underwear I assume that Spanish men really aren't packing very much downstairs.

It was the first night on the ship that I realized I could buy some clothes in the gift shop, they sold XXL shirts, underwear with American sizes and shorts.

The next day we landed in Alicante, Spain and no luggage was delivered. The next day we were in Cadiz, Spain then Lisbon, Portugal and still no luggage.

Five days had passed and the airlines had no answers. Everyone on the ship was fantastic in trying to help locate my luggage.

While in Lisbon I phoned my machine to check on messages. I had a message from United Airlines that they found my bag sitting behind the United counter at LAX with no destination tags on it. They were making a courtesy call to me to me know they had my bag at their baggage office.

I was thrilled to know that my bag was not lost but just lagging behind! I called Lufthansa with the help of the Crew Purser and they promised to overcome the issue of my being in a different port city each day. Our next few stops were going to be in France and England. I gave them every detail of my itinerary to overcome the possibility of missing the delivery of my clothes.

We stopped in Marseilles, France two days later. I was hopeful to get my bag but the French ship's agent told me there was no delivery.

I ventured into town to see Marseilles. I ran into passengers at a café and they invited me to sit down and have a drink. While we were chatting I looked over and to my shock and surprise I found a Big and Tall Men's store! I was so excited that I excused myself and ran over to the store.

I walked in and found a man sitting at a desk on the telephone. He smiled at me and I said, "Bonjour." I did not fool him and he immediately knew I was not French! He placed the phone down on the desk and walked over to me speaking French. I had no idea what he was saying and I just kept smiling! I figured this guy was going to make a big sale and I was going to have clean and fresh clothes to wear!

As I walked toward the rack of clothing I was cut off by the man on the phone who now seemed quite angry. I was more than a bit confused.

He physically helped guide me back to the front door of the business and proceeded to hustle me right out the door. He slammed the door shut, locked it and flipped the 'Open' sign to 'Closed'.

I stood there with my nose pressed up against the window in shock! What the hell just happened? I didn't say anything. I did not touch anything. I did not understand what was going on!

I knocked on the window as if to say, "Hey remember me?" He motioned for me to leave with his hand. I walked away dejected.

I returned to the café and the couple I was invited to join. They asked what happened and I why I had returned so quickly. I really did not have a good answer to that question.

So Marseille was very beautiful but I was still was without my bag, I had been kicked out of a shop in town and almost ripped off by a taxi driver. What a great day!

I stood outside the gangway to the ship having a smoke and keeping my fingers crossed that by the end of the day my luggage would be delivered. No such luck. I was feeling very down.

Two days later we were readying to leave Lisbon, Portugal. I was sitting in the crew bar when the Cruise Director walked in. He said that he had been looking for me to tell me my bag had been delivered!

I ran to my cabin with joy! There it was! I had never been so happy to see my luggage! I opened my bag and there was an explosion! My cabin was quickly engulfed. I was knocked off my feet not sure what happened. Until I began to be squeezed into a corner by a huge yellow life raft!

The Cruise Director, with the help of ship's engineers, rigged an inflatable raft to the zipper of my bag.

I heard the laughter outside my cabin door. The Cruise Director, Crew Purser and a few others were enjoying a laugh at my expense.

Practical Jokes

A South African crew member thought she was pregnant. She bought a home pregnancy test in a Greek pharmacy. She went to her cabin and took the test. She was trying to figure out the results but the box and all directions were in Greek.

I suggested that if she buys another test I would take it. I knew I was not pregnant. Then we could compare the strips and see if she was indeed pregnant.

That night after the crew bar closed I went into the bathroom and for the first time in my life I took a pregnancy test.

I handed off the little plastic case to the South African waitress and she started to cry. I was feeling really emotional. She could barely say the words, "Dave, I think you're pregnant!"

The girls who worked in the salons on the ships were all hired via an English company named Steiner. The girls who worked in the salons were referred to as Steiners. The girls are usually right out of beauty school in England and most were in their early twenties. This made them vulnerable to be on the receiving end of a lot of hazing.

Steiners were really great at initiating the new girls. They would give them a tour of the ship accompanied by a speech. They would educate the new girls about ship policy, all the great spots to shop and dine along the route the ship was taking.

Sharing of cabins was usually done by department. Steiners would bunk with Steiners. When the new girls would be assigned a cabin they would be handed a bill for electricity and water usage which had to be paid in advance or they would not be able to shower or have lights and air conditioning.

There are no written records of how many of the Steiners fell for that practical joke but I believe that the success rate was well over 95 percent!

I only participated in one such hazing. They had convinced a very sweet nineteen year old girl from the countryside of England that the ship insisted all new Steiners take a turn at Fog Watch. There was never a hesitation and almost never a question as to what Fog Watch actually entailed.

On her first night the new Steiner was issued a yellow raincoat, a bull horn and a whistle. She was instructed by the Spa Manager, a young lady from Belgium, that she was to man the bow of the ship from Midnight until 3:00 AM. She was also told if she spots any fog to immediately blow the whistle and announce on the bullhorn, "Fog Alert! Fog Alert! Fog Alert!"

The crew was buzzing with laughter and excitement as the young Steiner dressed in a yellow raincoat, in July, in the Mediterranean, where there is no fog in July, was readying to take her start on Fog Watch.

As I walked down the stairs to the crew bar she was walking up the stairs heading to the bow of the ship. I stopped and said hello, we had met earlier in the day, and wished her luck. I improvised on the spot and said, "I screwed up my first night on Fog Watch and we hit a small iceberg. I'm sure you'll do much better!"

At about 12:30 the crew bar emptied and everyone headed to the infamous Deck 11. Deck 11 was the highest point on the ship and only crew members could access the area. I was never going up there as my vertigo kept me from climbing the ladder.

I watched from another deck as this young Steiner diligently peered through binoculars on a beautiful and clear summer night. Two other Steiners snuck up on this young girl with sack full of flour and dowsed her in a fog of floating flour. Lucky for the new Steiner she was wearing a yellow rain coat for protection.

Tahiti to Helsinki and Beyond

When I arrived in Tahiti the Crew Purser told me that they were signing on new crew members and one of them was Manfred Kaineder! I knew Manfred well from other ships. I was excited to know at least one other crew member!

We were sitting in the crew bar in Tahiti. I said, "Manfred, do you know every ship I have been on you have also been there at the same time. The R2 on two occasions and the R5 and now we are together on the R3 smack dab in the middle of the Pacific Ocean in Tahiti."

Manfred sat up in his chair and said, "I have never been to Tahiti!" I busted out laughing since we were sitting right smack dab in the middle of Tahiti!

"You are here now!" I replied. Manfred literally had to take a moment to figure out where in the world he was. Manfred had worked 16 months with no time off flying from ship to ship reorganizing each ship's stock and supplies.

One night I was on my way back to my cabin and saw some of the waiters carrying sacks of potatoes. All the while they are laughing and shushing each other to keep the noise down. I stood there watching them as they placed one sack of potatoes after another in front of a crew cabin door. They stacked the sacks so high that they reached the ceiling.

They were giggling and laughing the entire time they were trying to be quiet. Manfred helped the waiters by opening the store room for them allowing them access to the potatoes.

Manfred told me that one of the waiters had been an asshole in the crew bar and got really drunk and that the alcohol magnified his being an asshole. To get even they decided to block him into his cabin with 1,000 pounds of potatoes preventing him from getting out.

I went to bed and I missed the payoff to the joke. The drunk waiter did not get up until late morning. I heard that he opened the door and 1,000 pounds of potatoes collapsed and caved in on him. He had a fractured elbow. Not all practical jokes end well.

One of the favorite practical jokes for the crew was to Saran Wrap the toilets in crew cabins. They would wrap it in such a way that the Saran Wrap could not be detected. A guy would go to the bathroom and wind up having pee splashed all over him and the bathroom.

Upon hearing that the crew members were participating in this someone suggested that they Saran Wrap the toilets in passenger cabins the day of embarkation. They would sneak into a cabin that was being cleaned by other stewards and wrap the toilet. The idea was that the steward for that cabin would not only have to clean up the mess but also have to explain to the Housekeeping Manager what happened.

This practical joke was very short lived. One steward got carried away and wrapped 25 cabin's toilets in Saran Wrap. All 25 cabins were under the watch of one steward. Before the ship even left port there were 10 complaints. The steward was called into the Housekeeping Manager's office to explain. He told the Manager that it was a practical joke that one of his coworkers had masterminded. They fired the poor bastard who wrapped the toilets and the Hotel Manager made sure no one had access to Saran Wrap again.

Stockholm Syndrome

Renaissance Cruise Line would employ a Broadcast Manager to handle all of the in house television and entertainment systems. On this ship was a particularly fun Broadcast Manager named Peder Pederson from Canada. Peder had a reputation at Renaissance Cruise Line as a fun loving hard drinking guy. He signed onto the ship and there was a buzz in the crew bar that Peder was back.

I met Peder his first night on the ship and Peder had shared that he left his credit cards and bank card back home with his Dad for safekeeping. It seems that Peder could not be trusted with his own money. He basically told us that he drank his income away from on last contract.

Peder was not handling the lack of cash well. He was borrowing money every night in the crew bar. He was budgeting himself so that he spent less than a $150 a week on partying. Seems like that would be an easy task to accomplish but not for Peder.

We were in Stockholm, Sweden doing a three night stay before heading to St. Petersburg, Russia where would spend four nights. A group of Steiners (the girls who work in the ship's spa), dancers, singers, pursers and one comedian headed into Stockholm for a night of drinking.

We settled into the first pub we found. I ordered a shot of Cuervo and the waitress asked how many 'mls' I would like. What in the world are 'mls'? She was asking me how many milliliters of Cuervo would I like. I did not know how many. She suggested 60 mls.

Well it turns out that 60 ml of Cuervo is a very large shot of Tequila! Not only was it large but expensive! I did not know that in Sweden there is a 25% Value Added Tax, a VAT. My shot of Cuervo was $40.00! Stockholm is a very expensive city!

At the rate we were drinking it was obvious that Peder was going bankrupt early! That would leave the rest of us to cover his bar tab.

Most people who have no money in their pockets will not order a cocktail at a bar. Peder believed that if he had no money in his pocket that someone would pick up his tab.

We moved on to the next bar at about midnight. We were getting really hammered. One of the Steiners was so drunk she peed behind a dumpster in the city center. One of the pursers was so drunk she left her shoes in one of the clubs.

By 12:00 in the morning Peder had been tapped out of cash and was wasted on beer and Aquavit. By 4:00 AM we were all buying drinks for each other and Peder was taken care of too. He was so well lubricated that Peder spied three pretty girls in the back of a taxi. He saw an opportunity and seized the moment. Peder jumped into the back of the taxi with the ladies. He began to introduce himself when three guys showed up. They were not at all happy to see Peder in the back of the taxi with their girlfriends. Peder very apologetically left the taxi before he could be physically handled. We stood on the curb laughing. Manfred, our ship's supply officer, yelled out, "You are now officially cut off! No more covering your bar tabs!"

Peder headed right into a phone booth next to the taxi stand. I thought he was seeking protection from the three guys in the taxi. Instead he was dialing his father in Canada.

I was standing there to make sure Peder did not get into any more trouble. I heard him talking to his dad and caught this classic line, "Hey Dad. I know I told you to not listen to me if I asked for my credit cards, but I need them right away! Can you send them Federal Express to Stockholm? Just address the envelope 'PEDER' Stockholm, Sweden. Renaissance Cruise Line R5."

Old Egyptian Man Teaches Young Jew About Tolerance

My most amazing experience that buoys my hope for a better world happened in Cairo in December of 2000. My then girlfriend and now wife, Ivy, was visiting me for a few weeks just before Christmas. It was the Islamic holiday Ramadan and the ship was spending the night in Alexandria, Egypt.

We hired a driver in Alexandria for a trip to Cairo and Giza to visit the pyramids my ancestors built. Ivy and I dragged our friend Dougie, the Crew Purser, along for the ride.

By hiring a driver and venturing out on our own we were warned of the dangers by everyone. There were several attacks on tourists in the area and they were well publicized.

Our driver, Mohammed, was a little Egyptian man with a bald head and stubbly trimmed mustache. He looked like my grandfather Manny. They were so similar right down to the tan Manny would have when he returned to New York from West Palm Beach. We decided to nickname Mohammed, Grandpa Mo.

The car we were taking through the desert on a two hour drive was a 1972 Datsun wagon. It was a jalopy at best. The tires were bald, the paint was faded and the backseat torn but the price was right.

The three of us loaded up into the car and off we went. We drove through Sadat City which was built to honor Egypt's greatest leader, Anwar Sadat. The city looked abandoned and decrepit. We drove past small towns and villages that were all poverty stricken and filthy.

The closer we got to Cairo the more traffic we had to deal with. Grandpa Mo was a champ at keeping us on the road. We all noticed how often he used the horn. It seemed as if the brake pedal may have been connected to the horn. There was endless cursing at other drivers and the whine of a 30 year old engine filled the car with unbearable noise.

I was fully aware of the poverty that surrounded us. Dougie and I were in Alexandria trying to avoid a local man selling papyrus prints. They were cheap, mass produced Egyptian images. Dougie was not interested in buying the papyrus but this man in a filthy traditional Egyptian suit started at $20.00. When Dougie showed no interest he lowered the price to $15.00 and then to $10.00 all the while he was following Dougie for almost one mile. Dougie eventually bought the collection of papyrus prints for $1.00! A man chased Dougie for 20 minutes and walked at least two miles back and forth from his little shop for $1.00. This was confirmation of the poverty we saw everywhere.

We got to Cairo and stopped at the Nile to take photos. We were in front of the Hilton Hotel which I thought would be a great place for lunch. Instead we opted for a McDonalds near Giza. We were the only diners in a city full of Muslims observing Ramadan.

We were being watched from the street as angry religious people did not appreciate our insult of eating during daylight in the holy month of Ramadan. To make matters worse we were smoking and drinking! I was wishing we had stopped at the Hilton instead.

After lunch we visited the famous Cairo Museum where King Tut is on display with all of his artifacts. It was amazing and breathtaking. The riches of a society that dated back 6,000 years were astonishing. Gold, lapis, onyx and more were turned into amazing works of art.

Egypt was one of the greatest empires ever known to the ancient world. They were sailors and navigated the oceans to conquer other nations. They were the most powerful country for centuries. Today they are in shambles. How could this happen? How could they fall so far after having so much?

We drove through Tahrir Square. There were buses with people stuffed into them and hanging out the windows. They were carrying live chickens and some were seated on the roof of the bus.

It was getting late and the sun was starting to go down. We were told by Grandpa Mo that it was time to go to the pyramids. He boasted that he would negotiate a great price for the camels for us to ride!

Ride a camel?! No way! I did that once in New York City when I was kid. It was one of the worst experiences of my life. I was afraid of heights and they throw me on a camel at a circus in Madison Square Garden. Suddenly the camel rises to what seemed to be 20 feet in the air. I cried. I never rode another camel and I would not ride one today.

In lieu of the camel we were driven to the pyramids on a horse drawn cart. The horse had gas! The worst gas you can imagine. It was even worse than the stench that hung over certain parts of the poverty stricken streets of Cairo.

As we galloped along the horse would fart. A rhythm had developed. Gallop...fart. Gallop...fart. We would laugh and shortly after we would be gagging.

Dougie was an old hand at riding camels. He lived in Dubai and quite enjoyed a camel ride. As our horse was trying to propel us faster with the aid of its natural gas Dougie was racing along side of us laughing as he too was being victimized by the horse.

We stopped at the pyramids. The overwhelming sense of sadness overcame me. This was a place where Jews were enslaved and even killed in order to build these great structures.

We did what all tourists do at the pyramids. We took photos of the three of us with our farting horse and Dougie's camel. We took photos of the Sphynx and eventually the sun went down and we left.

Grandpa Mo had one more stop to make. Like all good taxi drivers he had a favorite market to bring us to. Of course he was going to get a little kickback from the shop keepers for bringing us to them.

While wandering the market Grandpa Mo would follow us around encouraging us to spend money. Of course he had a vested interest in seeing us spend money as he would benefit from the sales.

Ivy purchased a few perfume bottles and some liquid incense or oil, as they called it. I picked up a few little carvings and stone pyramids. I knew that Jews did not build these pyramids and that was somehow satisfying to me.

As we wandered the market Grandpa Mo stopped me and pulled me aside near the opening of a tent. He grabbed my necklace which was dangling outside my shirt. He kissed my Star of David and tucked it into my shirt. He said he did not want anyone to see my Star of David and cause any trouble or injuries. He was genuinely concerned.

I was without words. Here was a little Egyptian man during Ramadan who was not only worried about our safety he was also so respectful that he kissed my Star of David! If any radical Egyptians would have witnessed that act Grandpa Mo would have certainly been in serious trouble right alongside of us.

That simple act of an Egyptian man kissing my Star of David was something that changed my life. I have ever since been more vigilant to never allow anyone to denigrate another for any reason.

To Russia with Love

The R5 was sailing the Baltic countries for the summer of 2000. I had signed on for the entire run and was thrilled to be stopping in St. Petersburg, Russia throughout the summer. The ship would overnight for four days at a time. It gives passengers extended time to enjoy the incredible amount of history and culture Russia has to offer.

On our first day in St. Petersburg the ship pulled into the closest port to the city center on the River Neva. We were walking distance to the Hermitage Museum which became my haven for the summer.

Each night before arriving in a new port the Cruise Director would give a lecture filling passengers in on what tours were available and what sites to enjoy. On this particular lecture there was a new subject I had never heard discussed before. The Cruise Director informed passengers to avoid eating hot dogs while in St. Petersburg. There were recent reports of people being ground into the hot dogs for consumption. Unimaginable! Yes! Why would the Cruise Director offer such gruesome information? While there was never any confirmation of such hot dogs being sold to passengers, there were hot dog vendors everywhere!

The first day in port I was standing on the ship's gangway when one of the ship's engineers, Jake, pointed out something floating down the Neva. I was not certain what I was seeing but with Jake's guidance I could make out a dead, bloated and naked body that was wrapped in rope. It was observed by the officers on the bridge and local police were called. The body floated past the ship and the Cruise Director, Craig, ran to the third deck to confirm that the body was indeed tied up in rope. Rigor mortis set in and the arms of the body almost looked like tree limbs floating in the river. The corpse was so bloated that it appeared to be a prop from a bad horror film. It was obvious to the tourists as well as locals that this was the work of the Russian Mafia.

Welcome to post communist Russia!

St. Petersburg is a magnificent city. The architecture dated back to the 1600s and some of the iconic Russian buildings were amazing. The Church Of The Spilled Blood, the Winter Palace, The Hermitage and more were just pictures in a book until now. This was the city my Grandfather was born in before immigrating to the United States. I felt a very strong connection.

There were brand new shops selling blintzes, borscht and stuffed cabbage. The tables were filled with pickles and cole slaw. The fear of eating a hot dog kept me dining in local restaurants where I could recognize the food without looking at a menu or a police report.

The night life was amazing! There were clubs and casinos that lined the Prospekt Nevsky, the main boulevard in St. Petersburg. The sun went down so late in the evening that on most nights we would leave to go out at midnight. Nights were filled with Vodka, beer, dancing and gambling. Some guys got so out of control that they were escorted back to the ship by the local police. Some guys acted out so inappropriately that they were locked up and left behind when the ship would sail off.

There was something about St. Petersburg that brought out the evil in a lot of really good people. Maybe it was the cheap vodka ($2.00 a bottle) or the high octane beer.
The first cab ride I took in Russia was to visit the Church of The Spilled Blood. The car was a little red Russian built car that looked to be 35 years old. There were dents, scratches, fading paint, bent bumpers and no signage that the car was actually a taxi. The more entrepreneurial Russians would hang out in the taxi line at the port and offer rides to the sites for a few dollars.

The driver was right out of central casting. He was huge, intimidating and looked very much like a Halloween mask.

There were giant scars all over his head and face. It was obvious that these wounds were not attended to by a doctor but rather sewn up with regular needle and thread. He looked like an extra from the movie Gladiator.

He spoke no English and my Russian was limited to vodka, blintz, borscht, nyet, and from watching Get Smart, KGB. I decided to just point at the spires as we drove across the bridge. It worked perfectly!

I spent a total of twenty nights and days in St. Petersburg. The vast majority of my time was spent in the Hermitage Museum. I would be in the museum by noon and on most nights I would leave by six in the evening. I saw the greatest works of art ever accumulated by a single entity. Degas, Renoir, Picasso, Van Gogh, Carvaggio, Botticelli, Michelangelo and all of the Dutch masters under one roof!

When I was a kid growing up in New York I loved art. Not just in magazines and museums but I loved the act of painting and drawing and being creative. Thanks to my junior high art teacher Dan Christoffel who nurtured and encouraged my art as a kid I was well aware of the privilege to be able to see these masterpieces live and in person.

The first original Leonardo da Vinci painting I ever saw was hanging in the Hermitage. I turned to see a glass case protecting the *Madonna and Child*. It was vibrant, beautiful and 500 years old. I literally cried as others tried to move me along so they too could enjoy the masterpiece.

At night the crew would finish their shifts and head into town in large groups. I was very friendly with the casino staff. One of the supervisors was a cat named Phil from England. He was a great guy with a great sense of humor and after hanging out with him for months I was able to understand most everything he said. Phil was great in St. Petersburg as he worked and lived there for a few years. He was running a local casino/nightclub called Hollywood.

Phil told me that the regular gang was going to the Hollywood Casino to party and gamble. I decided to leave later than everyone else and found myself standing in line at the casino. As I waited, two bouncers come to the velvet ropes next to me and opened the ropes so I could cut the line. I thought Phil had arranged for me to get in without waiting. I was escorted into the nightclub in the casino and was seated at a table by myself. As quickly as I sat down a silver ice bucket with a bottle of champagne was delivered to the table along with caviar and blinis. I tried to tell them I did not order the champagne or caviar but the waiter was very modest and insisted it was for me.

I sat there drinking champagne and eating caviar, which I loathe! Hey, I was in St. Petersburg and thought I would go all out. I kept looking around hoping to spy one of my friends. It seemed like I was sitting for way too long when Phil showed up.

Phil was talking to some of the casino people. They looked to be the guys who ran the operation. Phil was looking directly at me and nodding his head in my direction. He finally came to the table and sat down.

Phil said, "Dave you are going to love this one!" He was laughing and smiling and waving at the guys in the suits. He went on to share, "Dave, the guys over by the bar think you are a Russian mobster. They said you look just like a guy who gambled here when I was the manager. They wanted me to make sure you are treated like a VIP!"

I laughed and told Phil, "I guess we better tell them that I am not that guy."

Phil answered, "These are very serious mobsters who run this casino and I suggest you not say a word! Just play along and don't piss them off."

I was nervous and asked, "What if someone talks to me? What do I say?"

Phil said, "Don't say a word to anyone! Just sit here and in about twenty minutes get up and leave."

I did exactly what Phil told me to do. When I got back to the ship I waited for Phil to ask what the hell that was all about. Phil told me that I was a dead ringer for another guy and the fact that I was dressed like a Russian gangster did not help. I was wearing a black, doubled-breasted suit with a black shirt and a double-breasted, black overcoat! It must have looked as if Central Casting sent me out to read for the part of a Russian mobster.

Phil insisted that if I had told them I was not that *guy,* one of two things would happen. The first was possibly being tossed out on my ass and the second was more severe. Phil said, "Dave, we could have been the next two bodies floating down the River Neva or just more filler at the hot dog factory!"

Did I Just Say That?

After 25 years of traveling around the world I have logged three million frequent flyer miles, thousands of nights in hotels, hundreds of cruises and an untold number of laughs.

No matter how crazy or hectic my travels have been I have always seemed to be able to find something redeeming and worth laughing about. I have had my moments and there were many occasions where I acted less than civil to perfectly nice people and for that I apologize.

I was flying home to Los Angeles after four months of working in Europe. I was exhausted from a lack of sleep and way too much crew bar activity. I had been out partying with the crew from the ship and recovering from the Christmas and New Year's Eve holidays.

I reluctantly said good bye to all of my friends on the ship and headed to the airport in Athens. I checked in for my flight and inquired about using my stored mileage for an upgrade to first class. I was called to the desk at the gate and handed my first class upgrade!

I was so excited that my 8 hour flight would be in the luxury of first class! I was standing in the terminal giddy like a little girl! The flight was about to begin boarding and

I scored a ride up front! Then I heard over the public address system, "Mr. Goodman, to the podium. Mr. Goodman, to the podium."

I knew this was not good. I feared that my first class upgrade was going to be taken away. I approached the podium and the girl behind the desk said, "We are sorry, Mr. Goodman, we cannot accommodate any passengers in first class at this time. We will unfortunately have to move you to coach."

I was so depressed!

They allowed me to board the plane and I found my seat in coach. I was stowing my bag and getting comfortable when a middle aged woman with a small child sat across the aisle from me.

The woman was coaching her young child and encouraging him to have a seat. She was very vocal and continued to ask her son, "Benjamin, can you say seat belt? Benjamin, can you say armrest? Benjamin, can you say pillow? Benjamin, can you say flight attendant?"

I was, at first, impressed with her diligence but after a few minutes I was tired and annoyed by her diligence. All through the boarding process I kept hearing Benjamin's mom asking silly questions and in my head I kept hearing a voice saying, "Ha ha! You got stuck in coach! You got stuck in coach!"

Again I hear, "Benjamin, can you say flight magazine? Benjamin, can you say life vest?"

One more annoying question than the other and Benjamin never said a word! The kid must have been burnt out hearing his own mother's ridiculous questions.

I lost my seat in first class and now for the next eight hours I am stuck next to a woman who is going to narrate the entire flight for her kid, Benjamin.

I sat there getting angrier and angrier when I heard this, "Benjamin can you say..."

I snapped and said aloud, "Benjamin! Can you say, Mom shut the fuck up?!"

The eight hour ride to New York was very quiet!

I could not believe I said it. I was disgusted with my own behavior. I knew I had to apologize.

Eight hours later we landed in New York. I was waiting for my luggage when passengers started to approach me to thank me for keeping Benjamin's mom quiet! Apparently I was not the only passenger annoyed by Benjamin's mom.

Aruban Flag Day

In February 2000 I was flying in and out of Aruba for Carnival Cruise Lines Cruise Lines. I would fly in a day early and spend the night on the Island in one of the many budget hotels. They were always clean and always had great air conditioners! That's a big plus with Island humidity.

In April of 2000 I was super excited to be spending the night and being on the Island for the Flag Day Holiday. I was told that they held a Fat Tuesday Carnival like parade down the main street.

I landed at 5:00 in the afternoon and checked into my hotel. I caught a cab to the Crystal Casino and expected to have a five star dinner on the company tab. I found out that Flag Day was in full swing and all the restaurants were closed. Even the coffee shop in the casino was closed.

I was limited to one choice, McDonalds! Not much of a choice and not much a receipt to turn in for reimbursement. I was stunned at my bad luck.

I stood in the casino and decided a beer and a shot of tequila might help make my evening a little more tolerable.

I stood at a poker machine in the casino and put in my order. I pulled out my wallet and put a twenty dollar bill into the poker machine.

By the time I lit a cigarette and tipped the waitress I had noticed the lights blinking on the poker machine. I looked down to find the machine dealt me a Royal Flush. I hit the progressive jackpot of about $7,000.00.

I collected my cash in hundred dollar bills. I left the casino and headed down the stairs to the local McDonalds for my most favorite Quarter Pounder I ever ate! I kept my receipt and turned it in for reimbursement.

The next day the ship had stopped in Cartagena, Colombia. I ventured into town on a Sunday morning by myself. Not a great idea in Cartagena! I was immediately crowded by a group of salesmen trying to sell me phony Cuban cigars. I am way too schooled to be taken by the scam and the box of Cuban cigars I bought was just as phony as any of the others. I can admit it...I know that I'm vulnerable.

I jumped into a local jeweler that was open on a Sunday morning in a very Catholic country. They were catering to the cruise ship passengers. I found two members of the ship's lounge band buying Emeralds. I was not thinking about that when I left the ship! I just took my ID and some cash which I blew on phony Cuban cigars.

Pat, the guitar player in the band, was just finishing a transaction with the store owner. I asked Pat if I could possibly charge some stones on his card and give him the cash when we got back to the ship. Pat laughed and said he was at his limit.

The store owner said he would follow me back to the ship so I could get some cash for him. He allowed me to pick out a ring and a single stone. We negotiated a price that I thought was a great deal for me.

He followed me back to the ship and trusted me with the emeralds in my pocket to go back on board and get the cash to bring back to him. We were in a secure area guarded by Colombian Army soldiers. If I were a crook I could have easily remained on the ship and never returned with the money.

I walked off the ship to find the jeweler smiling and looking very relieved to see me again. I guess he was taking a chance on me when he gave me the emeralds. I walked right back to the fence and handed him the exact amount we spoke of. Through the small opening in the fence we shook fingers and said goodbye.

I Feel Like a MILLION EUROS!

I had been working for Renaissance Cruise Line and loving the people I was meeting and the experiences I was living. Every day we explored great cities and had new adventures. At night we would hang out in the crew bar. The laughter, the camaraderie and the people were amazing times.

Crew members were constantly signing on and off the ship. It was very sad to find that a crew member would end their contract and you would not have the chance to say goodbye. You would simply assume that you were going to see them again when they started their new contracts.

Just as I was finishing my longest contract at Renaissance Cruise Line a beautiful girl appeared in the crew bar in uniform. She was Canadian and well known by the Purser's staff. She had worked in the cruise industry for years and was engaged to another crew member on another ship for Renaissance Cruise Line.

Even though I was on the ship with her for few days we never formally met. I admired her fantastic smile and her conservative beauty. She really did light up a room. I signed off the ship never having been introduced.

Many months later I was signing onto the R3 in Tahiti. I had gone to the crew bar for a smoke and a diet Coke. I was one of only a few people in the bar at 1:00 in the afternoon.

I was waiting for my cabin to be cleaned so I could crash out and get some sleep after my flight. I was exhausted and I was falling asleep in the crew bar!

A few girls ran into the crew bar and immediately they all lit up. They sat across from me puffing and chatting. I was looking around to see if I knew anyone. I was looking for a familiar face to hang out with.

As I was nodding off and coming to I was introduced to the Cruise Director, Anthony. We stood in the bar talking and as other crew members entered the bar Anthony would introduce me to them.

Anthony would say, "Dave this is the Assistant Cruise Director Alexander. Alexander this Dave Goodman."

As Anthony introduced me to the next three or four people a young lady from across the bar walked over very cautiously. She got closer and asked, "Are you Dave Goodman? The comedian?"

I recognized her immediately! She was a beautiful Canadian girl with the most amazing smile! Her name was

Christina and she paid me the most amazing backhanded compliment.

Christina had told me that she was on the R5 just as I signed off in January of 2001. We met briefly on the ship but she made an impression. She worked with my good friend Dougie, the Crew Purser. She was on the R5 for a six month contract before going home to Canada to get married.

Christina told me right in front of Anthony, "You have no idea the affect you had on the crew members of the R5. One night after you left I walked into the crew bar. Dougie was sitting there with his regular crowd of mates. I sat there for about twenty minutes when I realized how solemn everyone was. I wondered why everyone was so quiet so I asked Dougie why."

Dougie told me, "Since Dave Goodman signed off the ship everyone has been really sad. Things have not been as much fun as when Dave was here!"

Confessions of a Cruise Ship Comedian

Taxis

When I was in Nice, France I shared a taxi to the ship with passengers I had met in town. We asked the driver how much the ride would cost prior to entering the taxi. We were told it was $20.00 American. Most drivers avoid using the meter. I assume it is because they are pocketing the money and not sharing it with the boss.

As we are getting close to the port the driver stops the car and tells us that he wants $40.00 for the ride. The couple I was traveling with said, "No way! You told us $20.00!" I took a quick look around to see where we were. I noticed that the road made a really sharp turn and right down the road about 1,000 feet was the ship!

I told the couple that the ship was right there and we could walk the rest of the way and we did. The best part was that the driver did not even get the $20.00 he originally asked for! He tried to screw us and in turn we screwed him! Boy does that feel great!

Rick Hardeman, my friend and musician from Renaissance Cruise Line, and I would entertain ourselves in cities we were visiting by going to lunch and window shopping. We ventured out in Athens for lunch but we made one huge mistake. We told the taxi driver we were going to lunch!

Of course the taxi driver tells us that he knows the best restaurant in Athens for lunch. Without hesitation the driver takes us to a little set of stairs in the midst of a commercial section of the marina in Piraeus. The driver told us to wait one moment and he scurried up the stairs returning a few minutes later.

He waived us over to the stairs and told us to enjoy our lunch. Rick and I were really skeptical. The restaurant was empty and there was no staff to speak of. There was just one gentleman with menus who welcomed us.

Rick said he would handle the situation. In his best southern voice Rick asked to see the menu. The gentleman holding the menus says, "Sir. We have no menus. We do a lunch special with fresh fish. It's the best in town!" The taxi driver confirmed the gentleman's statement. It was obvious at this point that the driver was getting a kick back for bringing us to his restaurant.

Rick insisted that he see a menu. He was not getting anywhere with this guy. Eventually Rick asked, "How much is lunch?" The gentleman stuttered, hemmed and hawed and finally said, "Only 28,000 Drachma per person!" The taxi driver shook his head as if to say, "That is a very good deal."

At the time the conversion was $70.00 per person!!! This was the land of the $3.00 gyro and this guy wants $70.00

for lunch! Rick cursed at the gentleman and told the taxi driver we wanted to leave.

The driver stood there motionless. He was not moving toward the taxi as we had hoped. He ran down the stairs and told us that he could not drive us anywhere since Rick insulted his friend.

Here we were in the middle of an industrial area of Athens we are not familiar with. We started to walk in the direction from which we came. After 15 minutes a taxi drove up behind us and out of the taxi came the driver who brought us to his friend's restaurant. He was shouting at us that we owed him money for the ride to the restaurant!

Rick argued with the man and I was afraid it was going to ramp up and turn into a street fight. Just as Rick was reaching his limit a police car stops to witness the action. The cops walk over and question the driver who was rambling on in Greek.

We were at a disadvantage not speaking Greek. The more the driver spoke the more I believed we were in trouble. Who knew what this guy was saying to the cops. Eventually one of the two cops slaps the taxi driver with an open hand. You could hear the pop of his hand as it hit the driver's face.

The driver jumped back into his taxi and drove off.

We walked for another hour before finding a taxi. Thankfully we were spared the trouble of continuing to walk in the wrong direction.

I love Greece but I hate Greek taxi drivers!

Ivy flew to Athens and we spent the day at the Acropolis. Late in the day we took a taxi back to the ship.

The driver did not know that I took the same drive back from the Acropolis a few times. It was roughly $4.00 in U.S. currency. This particular driver did not turn on the meter. Instead he turned on a timer which was measuring minutes and seconds. By the time we got to the ship the timer read "55555" which when converted to U.S. dollars was roughly $125.00!

This clown had enough nerve to try and rip me off! I was fuming but I kept my cool. As we were getting ready to leave the taxi I asked him to stop in the middle of the block and let us out. When he stopped the taxi I had Ivy get out and I handed the driver 1,600 Drachma which was exactly what I paid on all previous rides.

The street we were on was a very narrow one way street leading to the water. You could barely open the taxi door and have enough room to exit the cab. The driver started to yell and point at the meter while holding the 1,600 Drachma. He was motioning that I owed him more money.

I got out of the cab. There was a line of cars trapped behind the taxi with no ability to drive around. The line of cars were all honking and yelling at the taxi to move. He was torn between trying to rip me off and moving his cab.

The longer the scene played out the angrier I became. The taxi driver refused to move and now other drivers are exiting their cars to yell at him. The scene is getting more and more chaotic.

The driver got out of his taxi and I thought he was going to kick my ass! He was moving toward the passenger door that I had left open. He had to close the door in order to get through the streets of Athens. I assumed he was going to lunge at me so in a move to defend myself (and to teach the driver not to rip off tourists) I body checked the cab door like Bobby Orr playing the Rangers for the Stanley Cup. You could hear the hinges of the door pop and the crinkling of the metal.

I grabbed Ivy and we ran into Marks and Spencers, an English department store, and watched the scene play out from the safety of the store windows.

I had obliterated the door and it was not possible to close. There was no possibility of getting the car through the narrow streets with the door bent in an open position.

Ivy and I snuck out the other entrance and headed back to the ship. Once on board we were told that the ship was going to be leaving port late. Oddly enough, a tour bus full of passengers on a ship's excursion was stuck in a terrible traffic jam just outside of the port!

Made in the USA
Las Vegas, NV
23 September 2024

95677592R00103